Three Ladies, Three Lattes: Percolating Discussions in the Holy Land

Three Ladies, Three Lattes

PERCOLATING DISCUSSIONS IN THE HOLY LAND

Pamela Peled,

Tzippi Sha-ked,

Danit Shemesh

First published in the United States by Targum Publishers
An imprint of Renana Publishers

ISBN: 978-1-56871-579-7

Cover design: Diane Liff, D. Liff Graphics
Typeset in Garamond & Cronos by Raphaël Freeman, Renana Typesetting
Printed in Israel by Old City Press

www.renanabooks.com

Danit:

To my husband, my fellow sojourner in our odyssey to Truth.
To our children (Hila, Hadar, Harel, Hodee, Hodassa, Yehudit, Avigail, Ayala, and Batsheva) whom we invite with love to follow the path we paved.
To my father who believed in making a difference as we journey.
To my mother who believes in the difference I can make.

Tzippi:

To my dearest children:
Matan, Ciona, Tehila, Orie, and Chanan;
and my nieces and nephews –
I dedicate this book to you.
May your learning in yeshiva or university (ideally in both)
be an asset to Eretz Yisrael
and a blessing for our people.

Pam:

Martin –
if there was someone who could have brought world peace,
you were the one.
How I miss you, my darling.

Acknowledgments

Danit:

First and foremost I am most grateful to Hashem who orchestrated the universe in such a way that we three ladies can connect, merge our thoughts, and give birth to this book – an incorporation of polarized ways of life. I thank my dear husband, Yaacov, for his undying faith in Hashem, in Truth , in us, in me. May we be the wind beneath each other's wings until a very ripe old age. I thank my children for participating earnestly in the 'think tank' that was necessary for the process which culminated in this book. You are my inspiration, you keep me honest! I thank the Rabbis with whom I consulted and who supported this project, Rabbi Baruch Smith and Rabbi Moshe Mizrachi. You were my beacon of light when the darkness almost scared me right off this endeavor, making me want to recoil back into my haven of comfortable anonymity. I thank my dear friend and mentor, Shoshana Savyon, who has watched over and supervised my metamorphosis from cocoon to butterfly. I thank you dear ladies, my co-authors, for this super adventure and may it motivate others to join us with lattes!

Thank you Tzippi, my dearest friend, for seeing me through thick and thin, through secular and Haredi, for being there before marriage and nine kids ago, and dancing with me at my children's weddings even though you totally disagree with how I raised them. Thank you, Tzippi, for proving that friendship goes beyond *hashkafot*. When all is said and done, you and I will be old great-grandmothers together, still sitting around tsk tsk-ing about the state of affairs…

Tzippi:

The inspiration for this book came from my parents of blessed memory. They proved to me that a strong marriage can negotiate religious and secular terrain under the same roof and produce children with respect and regard for all types of Jews. To my Haredi brother and secular sister, your support and love mean so much to me. I wish we could model to others what our parents so successfully taught us: family is sometimes comprised of people with entirely different views, living harmoniously under a common roof.

I want to thank my wonderful partners in this project: Pam and Danit. You've been intrepid and inspiring co-travelers on this wonderful journey, teaching me many things. My loving children who've cheerfully put up with my numerous projects, I thank you for all of your support – you are simply my fuel. To Madlibs, thanks for your vote of confidence, your insight, and the many hours you spent helping us find the right publisher. Finally, I thank my husband for giving wings to all of my projects. You're simply the best...

Pam:

A number of years ago a beautiful, pensive student joined my editing course at Beit Berl College in Israel. She had hardly been in any lessons before she started steering the class into discussions on difference, and tolerance, and cheering up the world. That student was Tzippi, the powerhouse behind this project, and one of the most caring human beings I have ever known. How lucky I am to have encountered her on this earth, and how lucky that she introduced me to Danit.

I have been blessed in this life: my perfect parents gave me the strength to go placidly amid the noise and the haste, and to negotiate the drama of life without crutches. My family, all of them, make up a tight net under the shaky rope we all walk each day. Martin, my beloved husband, was not spared to see this work in print; he edited it in his normal brilliant manner, and he encouraged me to participate in the book, as he encouraged me to breathe in and out. My beautiful daughters – Sidelle, Tal and Joanna – give me a reason to smile each day; they are my inspiration and prove to me that with all the sham, drudgery and broken dreams, this is still a beautiful world.

And Israel... I would not have been half the thinking person I am today without the journey of many years in this challenging, lovely land. I might have had less wrinkles... but who cares about wrinkles?

Contents

INTRODUCTION
Three Lattes, Please xi

CHAPTER ONE
The First Cup of Latte: Making our Acquaintance 1

CHAPTER TWO
Why We Love Israel 13

CHAPTER THREE
Cross-Dressing in Israeli Society: A Core Struggle with Sexuality, Nidda and Hair Covering 22

CHAPTER FOUR
Keeping the Faith 42

CHAPTER FIVE
Sex in the Small City 55

CHAPTER SIX
A Jewish Mother in Israel 73

CHAPTER SEVEN
What we Know to be Treif: The Ladies Air out Communal Dirty Laundry 86

CHAPTER EIGHT
Paralysis? Army/Work/Politics 102

CHAPTER NINE
Mental Hygiene for the Jewish Soul: A Prescription from Three Maidels 133

CHAPTER TEN
Very Caffeinated Questions for the Three Maidels 161

Appendix 1 181
Epilogue 183
Glossary 185

Introduction

Three Lattes, Please

"Either write things worth reading, or do things worth writing."
Benjamin Franklin, *Poor Richard's Almanac*

Pam writes:

Café Café in the city of Modi'in's spanking new mall might not be one of the world's best coffee shops. But it could well be one of the few overlooking a city that sprang up from a desolate space in less than two decades; a thriving mini-metropolis which boasts a lake and rowing boats, and a super-modern train station. Modi'in has been carefully planned to incorporate green spaces and fun places; their foundations have been sunk into ground near where the ancient Jewish Hasmonean dynasty ruled Judea over a millennium ago.

Modi'in has seen its share of action. In 167 BCE, for reasons that have been lost, the Greeks, who were ruling Israel at that point, forbade Jewish sacrifice. For good measure they banned the celebration of Sabbath and Festivals, and outlawed circumcision. Altars to Greek gods popped up in strange places, complete with sacrifices of pigs (prohibited, of course, to Jews.) Zeus, the Olympic God of War, was plunked down on the altar of the Jewish Temple. The Jews were prepared for only so much of this behavior. A year later they revolted, led by Mattathias the Hasmonean, a Jewish Priest from Modi'in.

So the coffee shop in the mall comes with quite a history. But history was not what was bothering me on a balmy early autumn day in October, as I waited to meet my coffee dates. Tzippi I already knew: her energy, warmth, and positive outlook on difference reassured me that the project we were about to undertake was 'do-able.' But Danit was the wildcard – all I knew was that she was originally Californian, and Haredi. Now here's the thing: I'm scared of Haredim. I'll share these fears; for the moment I'll just quote Moshe. Moshe is our taxi-driver; he drove my husband to the airport a few hours before the first working meeting for this book. Moshe was crying, my husband reported later, on the phone from Europe. As Moshe negotiated the pre-dawn, deserted roads he bemoaned his fate: two of his sons are now Haredi. He supports them, and all their kids. They don't work (too busy studying Holy Texts), and they have many, many kids. Moshe put his retirement plans on hold and worked nights, instead of days. The kids kept coming, and the sons kept studying, so Moshe began to work nights and days. Now he takes food to his children, who live in dingy apartments, and they thank him and ask him to dress more modestly when he delivers it. Moshe loves his boys, but he doesn't know how much longer he can cope.

I was thinking about Moshe as I prepared to meet Danit. I was expecting – I'm ashamed to say it, but there you go – I was expecting a washed-out, haggard mother-of-nine, with dark rings under her eyes and a shapeless skirt hiding a tummy that had been stretched over and over and over and over and over again. And then some. I was expecting "*Baruch Hashems*" and "*Be'ezrat Hashems*" and I was certainly expecting a freezing reaction to my point of view. But Danit disarmed me.

Danit is gorgeous. Her warm eyes sparkle under her scarf-swathed hair, and her skirt flows over a well-toned body. She laughs infectiously at opinions that should outrage her; and says "I love it!" astonishingly, and often. Tzippi sits there emanating her calm, beautiful karma; her long, dark (artificial) hair framing her model's face. We talk, and laugh, and talk and talk some more. And I sit there too, drinking my latte, and feeling my fears wash away with the warm milk. We can do this, I think.

We can present our viewpoints.

We can discuss.

We can disagree.

And we can remain friends.

And maybe we can even influence each other, at least a little, to embrace new ideas and understandings.

Let's see...

Tzippi writes:

> *"... It is proper, out of love of reason and knowledge, that you not {summarily} reject anything that opposes your own ideas, especially so if {your adversary} does not intend merely to provoke you, but rather to declare his beliefs... For the proper way to attain the truth is to hear {others'} arguments which they sincerely hold, not out of a desire to provoke you. Thus it is wrong simply to reject an opponent's ideas; instead, draw him close to you and delve into his words... "*
>
> Maharal, Rabbi Judah Low Ben Bezalel, of Prague*

My 11-year-old son, Orie, came home late from his Saturday afternoon *Bnei Akiva* Youth Group meeting. He was hot and sweaty, and nearly melting from the Mediterranean sun. Still, he had a thoughtful expression on his sweet face.

"What's up, *Motek*?" I ask.

"Well, we got our new club leaders today and it was so, so, so hot but they had an interesting *peulah*," he answers, plopping down on our brown leather sofa.

"Oh yeah? What about?" I was setting the table for the next Sabbath meal, but I took a break to join him on the sofa.

"Well, Menachem, our *madrich*, asked how we would set up a new community in Israel. He gave us options, and told us to pick four very important people."

"You had to name the people?" I ask.

"No, just what they do for a living. Our choices were a rabbi, a plumber, a soldier, a doctor, a carpenter, you know, people like that," Orie answers.

"So what did you say?" I run my hand through his curly hair.

"A soldier, a doctor, a farmer, and a rabbi," he says. "All my friends answered differently."

---

* "Be'er HaGolah", translated by Dr. Norman Lamm, Torah Ummada, Jason Aronson, pp. 57–58

"Did Menachem like your answers?" I am curious.

"Well, sort of. No, not really. Actually he made us think hard. He said I picked good people, but what about a plumber? How would we have running water so the farmer could grow things? He asked Yossi, who didn't pick a soldier, if his community would feel safe. It was like that for everyone. Everyone chose good people, but there was always someone missing."

"So what did the activity mean to you?" I wait to gauge if he'd had an epiphany.

"I learned that when you start a village, it takes a combination of people to make it work. Everyone has a different job, and each is very, very important. No job is more valuable than another. Life wouldn't be the same with any piece missing. Menachem says this is true of Jews too. We have to work together; you know what I mean, Mommy?"

I smile. I know exactly what he means. I provide a Jewish analogy: "Say, Orie, that you were a secular, out-of-work plumber. You don't think so highly of yourself, or even know where you fit into society. At eight in the morning, in the synagogue down the street, nine important religious rabbis are gathered for *Shacharit*, the early morning prayers. The problem is that for a *minyan*, a prayer quorum, you need ten men. It would be up to you, Orie, to be that tenth man. They can't launch their prayers to God without you. You, the secular Jewish plumber, are just as important as any of these rabbis when it comes to prayers being heard. This is what Jewish unity is about."

Orie nods his head, a satisfied smile on his lips.

Easier said than done – this Jewish unity business. A friend warns me this project will be an exercise in futility; or a sure-fire way of losing two friendships.

I am naive. I ignore her. Here is my idea:

With so much about Israel/Diaspora relations hitting the headlines, I want to probe internal Jewish relations among women right here in Israel. This seems straightforward enough. I will recruit two friends from across the religious spectrum, steadfast and entrenched in their convictions. We'll meet once a month over Lattes, and discuss pressing topics. We'll research whether three Jewish women, from disparate backgrounds, can have a meaningful dialogue on issues that polarize our society. We'll examine whether we can respect each other, and refrain from the blame-game, despite our diametrically opposed views.

We all like Lattes, and chocolate; we'll choose a coffee shop to play a pivotal role (not only on our hips.) We'll meet, and chat, and try not to criticize nor convince, but rather to converse. After all, as Rabbi Dr. Nathan Lopes Cardozo notes:*

> "Human experience shows that as long as two people do not physically meet, look each other in the eye, and see each other smile, they often develop wholly mistaken impressions of their opponents. In that case, an important component for proper dialogue is missing. One should, after all, never forget that the success of a dialogue is not only dependent upon the strength of the speaker's argument, but also on the purely physiological impressions that they convey: such as a smile, a laugh, or even the way one sits, how one looks at the opponent, and how one lifts one's eyebrows."

I'm not seeking coherent theological responses from Pam or Danit, but rather constructive dialogue. So, in a miserably hot and humid Israeli summer, an idea was born. Pam and Danit seem natural partners.

While the three of us realize that inner-faith-based relationships may be unsolvable, we will give the '*other*' the benefit of the doubt, and listen. I know my optimism might be sorely tested. I know I may lose hope of bridging or healing the gaping 'Jewish divide.' I pray that this project will not grind down two friendships.

Jews and Judaism are complicated subjects. While Israel is a democracy that embraces freedom of religion, religious practice is, or should be, our collective responsibility. As an Israeli citizen, I may have a civic responsibility to get along with other members of society, but as a Jewess, I sense a moral imperative to reach out to my fellow Jew. Still, in some respects, I feel that Pam, Danit, and I are stepping into a sparring ring. Squaring off in the red corner is Pamela Peled: attractive, unabashed, strongly principled, smart, dynamic, Zionistic and Jewishly defined, antinomian in halachic spirit and practice. Pam's infectious spirit shouts out: I am Jewish, proud, culturally centered but I will live my Jewishness

---

* Cardozo, N. *Thoughts to Ponder*, Jerusalem: Urim Publications, 2005, p. 26.

my way, on my terms. Let no man, or no orthodox understanding of God, define my parameters, my comfort zone.

In the blue corner, making her way just as intrepidly to the center ring, with *kashered* gloves, vibrant eyes, and an indomitable spirit is Danit Shemesh: mother of nine, free-spirited artist, wielding a masterful paintbrush that touches many lives and canvases; Haredi by choice, confident, and proud of her Jewish skin. She brings an energy that may leave us exhausted. Danit reads global and local temperatures and synthesizes micro and macro realities through Torah-filtered lenses. And she never, ever, lets annoying facts get in the way of her positions.

Both ladies, slight in figure though never light in their views, ensure my work is cut out for me. While the project is my idea, I've begun to question my role. The problem is that I see both sides of the story. I can relate to both women's world views. Where does that leave me? Will I be too busy playing 'moderator' between polar positions to get my own voice across? Will I be a facilitator; a bridge across troubled waters, or (gulp), a toreador between Haredim and their opponents? After only one meeting, I sense I might have to be a balm between two cogs grinding on each other. I'm caught between two red-heads and I only foresee red: red heifers charging in a fragile china shop of budding inner-faith friendships. *Gevalt.* One thing's for sure, I needn't worry that either lady will ever feel inhibited to speak her uncensored mind. G-d help us.

Danit writes:

Tzippi and I go back a long way – she is my oldest friend of close to thirty years. We've been discussing existential issues and solving the world's problems forever. Or rather *she* solved world crises while *I* was mesmerized by the fascinating turn of events she unveiled for me. Tzippi is my Cliff Notes. When I first met her in the university elevator, I knew this girl was no ordinary ditz; she was a Woman With A Mission. I was dazzled by her stubborn persistence that there was a better way, a formula for living, a method to the madness. Me? I just went with the flow and lived in the moment. While I wondered what to wear to a party, she made lists of books to read. After we both married and bore children, I was reduced to putting out fires and creating coping mechanisms. Tzippi, on the other hand, planned educational curriculums and made New Year resolutions…every month. She knows how one *must* live one's life. Me? Well, I am still dog-paddling along, hoping not to get too wet.

When Tzippi shared the idea for *Three Ladies, Three Lattes*, I was like a deer caught in the headlights. At first I declared I had nothing to say. I just work here. Every day is an adventure for me; every day feels new and raw. I am in a life with wall-to-wall kids who call me '*Ima*' and expect food, clothes, and education. I am 'modestly' covered from head to toe. I live in a place where all men wear black. In our community it's a joke to point out a husband as 'the one with the beard' as every man sports one. My boys attend a *yeshiva* in Bnei Brak and expect to marry women who will financially support their learning. My oldest daughter married via a *shidduch*. It's a rare treat for me to sit with my husband at a wedding. I don't remember signing up for this, but here I am. I can't represent Haredim; I am a mere cog in this well-oiled machine.

My son told us about a boy and his father who go out walking. The son asks, "Dad, why is the sun yellow?" The father answers, "I don't know." The boy ponders and asks, "Dad, why are Indians called 'red'?" The father doesn't know. The boy continues, "Dad, why are there twenty-four hours in a day?" The father shrugs. The boy sighs, "Dad, does it bother you that I ask so many questions?"

The father smiles. "No, son," he says, "how else would you know the answers?"

So, I will try to answer your questions, accusations, or complaints as this cog. Anyone who knows Tzippi, knows she is 'The Great Persuader.' When I first saw the spark in those wonderful brown eyes, accompanied by "I have an idea!" I ducked. That's the only thing to do when she has an epiphany. But I ducked in vain.

Then I met Pamela. Leave it to Tzippi to bring in the big artillery. Tzippi warned me not to be late, which, of course, I was. (I had good reasons: a sick child, a husband who needed the car, and a meeting with a teacher of yet another child.) I came to Pamela with my breath in my hands, trying to make a good impression without letting her know that my tardiness is always due to numerous young people in my life. My fear was hearing the usual "well-you-asked-for-all-of-those-kids; you-got-them."

With Pam, I loved her smile. It put me at ease immediately; no simple task. In time, when we rolled up the ole' sleeves, I was still deceptively at ease; she had her opinions which did not infringe on mine. Her outlook on life was simply different, even diametrically opposed from mine, and yet, I was still standing, unmoved from my views. Then Pam announced that she would prefer her daughter married a non-Jew than a Haredi Jew. What could I do? She was entitled to her opinion, even if it made me itch. Her position did not threaten mine, even if it purported to do just that.

There are a number of players on this playing field called Israel, and each is equally important. Perhaps Tzippi is right; it's time to co-exist instead of 'one-upping' each other. Still, as our project unfolded, it became clear that we were not talking *to* each other, but *at* each other. Very rarely does a person genuinely take into account what the next person is thinking. Sadly, it seemed that we were using each other to get our own points across, to understand ourselves better, instead of understanding each other.

I was born secular and happily held onto my views for my first twenty-six years. I know the party line on freedom and feminism, and I may even agree with a lot of what my sisters in the larger community say. Pamela made a wonderful impression; she is a lady of character and elegance, feminine and strong, all rolled up into one small, beautiful body. Yet, she struck me as still another voice in the cacophony of Haredi-bashers. In her refined South African accent and with impeccable grace, she casually informed me that she considers my neighbors and me 'a threat to her existence.'

What led to my light bulb moment was that despite her intelligence and mild-mannered composure, she still spewed out the same-old-same-old.

I, as a Haredi woman, am woefully misunderstood by the larger society. It is not anyone's fault. It feels uncomfortable to me to be breathing the same air, on the same land, with sisters who misread me so enormously. Being an artist and a free spirit in the Haredi world, I am somewhat of an enigma. As I listened, something inside me clicked. It was time to speak my piece, because I have what to say. I don't represent the whole Haredi world; how could I? I just live here. I don't represent

G-d. That's for the Rabbis. I merely articulate one Haredi woman's perspective on living in Israel.

As a Haredi woman, I don't merely do as I am told and shut up. I have a voice. I do what I believe is right; I pro-actively choose to be Haredi and to bring up my children in this community.

I am not here to solve a global problem, sorry Tzippi. I am not here to allay and appease Pamela's concerns. Sorry Pamela. I am here to introduce another voice. Behind the beards and hats, behind the scarves and pregnant bellies there is a voice, rich with conviction, and determined to live right. Behind the 'extremism' and separatism there is a voice: authentic and spirited, inspired and caring, genuine and loving.

What does it mean to have Haredi, *Leumi*, and secular communities? Is it akin to opposing Indian tribes who fight each other to the death for a piece of land? Is there a Queen of Hearts on her throne yelling, "OFF WITH THEIR HEADS!!?"

Hardly.

We are one big family which needs to realize that we are in this together. No one is going to change their mind and go elsewhere. So . . . now what?

It is said that if you want to capture someone's attention, whisper. I am whispering from my tiny neck of the woods. I don't believe Pamela and I will ever agree, or even Tzippi and I. That is not my intention.

The message that my voice will sing out is that there is another, less accessible piece to this intricate puzzle of life: the G-d piece. The Haredi community tries to live the expectations of G-d through Torah teachings. This world is made up of the physical and measurable, as well as the metaphysical and the immeasurable. My voice speaks forth from the second level. We search for a place where we understand ourselves in relation to the infinite, not to the physical. The search for grace, infinity, love, and true peace lies in the metaphysical.

Names in Hebrew represent their essence. Take 'Cain' and 'Hevel.' 'Cain' means acquisition. He placed great importance on the material. That was fine at first as he was given prosperity; however, he got greedy, and didn't want to hand anything over to G-d. His brother 'Hevel's' name means futile: the material world had no meaning for him, apart from being something to give to G-d.

An equally polarized pair of brothers is Eisav and Yaacov. 'Eisav' is rooted in 'Asui,' a finished product formed to fit the material world. The Torah calls him *ish* (man) from the minute he was born (with teeth and hair, like a grown man.) He was *ish ha sade*, or 'man of the field,' a huntsman. He relished physicality; he was born the king of the castle and had no notion of the metaphysical. Yaacov (meaning 'heel') was born just behind Eisav, holding his heel. Yaacov did the bare minimum to live in this world; he was *ish tam* (a man of integrity.) His mouth (which symbolizes managing in this world) and his heart (the spiritual/metaphysical) were one. He was complete, and inward seeking.

A sculptor is called a *mephasel* in Hebrew, from the word *psolet* meaning extraneous. Allow me to be a sculptor and release the excess, so as to make us more understandable.

May G-d put the right words under my fingertips because I surely cannot do this without Him.

Chapter One

The First Cup of Latte: Making our Acquaintance

Pam writes:

OUR FIRST COMMUNAL CUPPA

The summer of 2010 was one of the hottest on record; the air was almost too heavy to breathe. The only way to stay sane was to hang about inside with the air-conditioning turned way down low, or plunge into the nearest swimming pool. I am blessed in this department; courtesy of my handy husband who mail-ordered a kit and assembled it single-handedly, I have a perfect plastic pool in my back yard, complete with a surfer's rope tied to the deck. We loop this contraption around our waists and swim for hours, anchored in the center of the water, going nowhere fast. We can float on blow-up mattresses, reading the paper or snoozing in the sun, feeling cool.

One of my favorite summer pastimes is brunch in bikinis – minus the bikinis. As my friends and I have grown older and saggier, and as waxing, tweezering, and shaving just seem an unnecessary effort, our bikinis have given way to full-piece swimsuits, often covered by baggy t-shirts that hide what should not be flaunted. But we clamber onto the airbeds year after year, closing our eyes behind sunglasses as we sip white wine and talk about our growing kids, and our growing list of medical conditions, and our growing sense that life is so sweet, and so short.

But this year, on one brutally boiling day, I shocked myself. It happened during a particularly pleasant brunch: delicious home-made granola and oven-baked cranberry bread, fresh fruit salad and ice-cream to scream for, strong milky coffee drunk while we were dripping wet. We were giggling, my friends and I, over some silly remark, and the talk turned to our kids and what we wished for them. Friendship was high on the list, and a good education, and health, of course, and health. Some money wouldn't hurt, we agreed, on condition that we all had our health. And love, we said. We want good husbands for our gorgeous girls; good wives for our lovely sons. And health.

Then I surprised myself. "As long as they don't come home with Haredim," I heard myself proclaiming. I stopped, astonished at what I hadn't even known I felt.

"What?" challenged one of my friends, whose sister was a born-again Haredi, with countless kids and a husband who studied (and didn't work.)

I sipped my coffee and thought long and hard. My crystallizing thoughts smashed down hard on my normally well-toned equilibrium. Honest to God, I discovered there and then, I would much rather my daughter stood under the *chuppa* (or didn't) with a non-Jew, than next to a man swimming in a black gown, or a white bathrobe-like kittel, who was forbidden to kiss her after he shattered the ceremonial glass. Hands down, I'd go for a nice young Brit who had never met a Jew before, or an Australian pianist, or doctor, or judge, or a South African tennis player perhaps – someone with whom we could converse, and take to the beach, and visit on Shabbat. A man who would create children with my daughter, and educate them to be self-sufficient; to work, to play, and to go to the army. A Haredi husband would stuff my grandsons under big black hats, and not teach them maths or English, or football, or how to swim. A Haredi husband would want multiple children, and expect my husband to support them (unless his parents were not ultra-religious either, and could share the financial burden.) A Haredi husband would not consider the army for his sons, and never, God forbid, for his daughters. Competitive *kashrut* would compel the home – how many hours do *you* wait between meat and milk? Which meat is *kosher lemehadrin* deluxe? Please, I prayed to God, anything but a Haredi husband for my girls.

I didn't like this attitude. I didn't like myself for feeling so *hard-koppig* as my late dad used to say – so dogmatic, so intolerant, so incensed. I am a proud Jew. I resolved to come on *aliya* at the age of ten; I moved to Israel two weeks after High School. I love it here. I grew up going to synagogue every week, Friday nights and Shabbat, and leading the Children's Service for years. We keep a kosher kitchen in our home near Tel Aviv, and we light Shabbat candles, and wash our hands before the Friday-night meal. We do the blessing on the ablutions, and then we bless the bread, and my husband blesses all the kids. We gather in the living room, my husband, my girls, and me, prior to every overseas journey, and we ask God to guide "our going out and our coming in from this time forth and forever more." We fast on *Yom Kippur,* and we change our plates for *Pesach*, and we build a *Succa* and sit in it.

I like Judaism; I like being Jewish.

So what's with the Haredim?

Here's the thing: I slip between the streams of Judaism in Israel. Abroad, in South Africa, where I grew up, you could drive to *shul* on Shabbat, pop your *kippa* on your head, *daven* away with the best of them and then, fortified with some fish cakes and chopped herring from the *Kiddush,* head over to the Jewish golf-course for eighteen holes. Judaism was belonging; it was community, it was home. In Israel, you are religious – or you aren't. You have to identify: you cover your head, or you don't. If you cover, there's more categorization: are you a wig-woman, a hatter, or a twister of scarves? If you watch TV on Fridays, after the witching sunset hour, then you have no place going to pray. If you don't haul yourself out of bed to join a morning *minyan,* you are a man who should eat pork chops fried in butter.

Outside of Israel the edges are gentler; you meld more between the lines. You can go bareheaded by day, but hat-up for Friday night services. You can keep kosher at home, but eat anything out. It just works like that. Each to their own, and all together.

In Israel the question of Shabbat is existential. It's not each individual who chooses whether to catch buses to the beach on the Day of Rest; the Government decides if public transport will run. Today's drama is whether Income Tax Internet Sites and VAT pages should be closed on Saturdays, so the less pious in the country can't sin by clearing debts during sacred seconds. The Government almost fell once when a prime minister ordered electricity turbines moved in the dead of night on

Shabbat, when they would least disrupt Israel's notorious traffic. It did fall one fateful year, when the national airline landed after Shabbat 'came in.'

Because there is no separation of religion and state, halachic laws govern marriage and birth and death. Women whose husbands refuse to divorce them are chained by religious laws to a life lived as captives; they have no recourse to a civil court. Non-Jews cannot marry Jews in Israel and be recognized as legally wed; non-Jews can't be buried in local cemeteries even if they died in battle for the country. Unless you are one of the very religious, or you just don't think much, you have to feel edgy with these issues.

But, you say. Okay. It's a Jewish country, and these are the Jewish ways. We'll learn to live with them; find a modus vivendi. We *want* the country to close down on *Yom Kippur*; it's atmospheric that supermarkets banish all breads for the *Pesach* week. That's what makes Israel Israel, like pomegranates at the start of the year, and oily donuts at Hanukka. Fair enough – we can work it out.

But then there's the big bad humdinger that clonks you on the head when you think of Haredim, and it's not their quaint clothing or downcast eyes in the presence of women. Haredim take the Biblical injunction to "be fruitful and multiply" literally; they have up to ten children at the drop of a *tallis*, and often many more. But here's the rub: Haredi men normally don't work. Haredi men pride themselves on being scholars; they spend years and years and more years in *Yeshivot*, learning, learning, learning. Much of their intellectual pursuit centers on the Bible; stories of lust, revenge, and sexual proclivities ranging from incest to rape. Some studies focus on how to have relations with one's wife; how to stimulate her and when to pray, how to know whether she is clean enough for action. Young boys study these subjects in a vacuum; it is unheard of to experiment with the opposite sex; even looking at them languidly before marriage is utterly taboo.

That's tough for them; but why should I care?

I'll tell you why: I pay for these studies. Yeshiva *bochers* get a stipend for sitting and boning up on King Solomon's concubines; how many he had, what he did with them, and why he was punished. My kids pay for the privilege of learning mathematics, and physics, and statistics, and

French. They pay to be lawyers, and dentists, and teachers. They clean tables at night, or sell perfumes in malls, or work as guards all weekend, to subsidize their studies. And their taxes go to pale-faced boys in large black hats who sit in study halls for years, being pious.

There's another thing. Our kids go to the army; girls for two years, boys for three. Sometimes they sign on for more time, as officers and captains. My own three girls did a year of service before they joined up for military service; volunteering with underprivileged youth and running programs to improve the society in which we live. Without getting paid a penny. My brother was wounded in Lebanon. My husband, who came to Israel when he was thirty-five, did target practice for a week and was shipped off to Nabatiya, leaning out of trucks with his rifle at the ready, not sure what he'd do if he had to shoot.

The Haredim, by and large, do not consider defending their country as their duty. Less than one percent of the pious join the army. *Moshe Rabbeinu*, our greatest sage, did his fair share of fighting, even if it was just urging on his troops when the going got tough. King David fought the Philistines, and *Yeshivot* examine glorious bestings of Amalekites and Hittites by the Hebrews of old. But the wimps of today don't believe in battling; not when some other suckers can do it instead.

Here's the problem that impacts on me: this year, 2012, fifty percent of Israel's first grade students are either Haredi or Arab. Neither group goes to the army; both groups are challenged in the employment arena. Arab women by-and-large don't work; neither do Haredi men. The Arab birthrate is 2.5%; the Jewish 1.7%. But the Haredi school system is growing at a rate of 39 times more than the secular schools; Haredim weigh in with up to 15 or more youngsters per household. Secular Israelis generally have no more than two kids, or three. Very, very soon the majority of our society will be non-sustainable; I will be sustaining them. Me, my husband, my children, and the dwindling number of the working world here in this ancient land; while the Haredim pray for our souls and make sure that no drop of *chametz* gets in the *Kosher-le-Pesach* soap powder.

It's a sobering thought, no?

Tzippi writes:

WOMEN DO NOT LIVE BY COFFEE ALONE: HAVE A ROGELACH . . .

For Pam, Haredim are not merely a demographic threat, but a doomsday scenario. They give her a headache. Danit agrees existential peril hovers overhead, but she believes it emanates from secular sectors. Here is my view: born and raised in smoggy, Hollywood–drenched Southern California, I hail from an unconventional yet 'traditional' family. We kept Shabbat and *kashrut*, and as many other commandments as possible. My father, (may he rest in peace), was knowledgeable in Jewish affairs, with a decidedly secular bent. My mother, (may she, too, rest in peace), leaned towards Torah observance, yet warmed to people of all faiths. My parents' marriage was an artful negotiation of Californian-chilled mores and religious principles, all observed while keeping their children relatively sane. My folks represented a 'meeting of hearts.'

As their daughter, a wife and mother of five wonderful children, a teacher and champion of Jewish ideals, I view myself as a seeker. A religious Jew, I still experience bouts of existential angst and shed tears at man's ultimate loneliness. Being a believer with a certain level of doubt is a balancing act I find strangely comforting. So, while I despair at the increasing lack of Jewish unity, I remain stubbornly hopeful that something can be done.

It is certainly challenging negotiating one's space on the Israeli religious turf, where every inch is symbolically 'staked.' Caught between secular and Haredi coordinates, it's small wonder many new *olim* view the middle path – Modern Orthodoxy – as the most inviting Torah road. (A disproportionate number of North American families who have made *aliyah* since 2002 are from Modern Orthodox homes.)

But I'm not here to sell you Modern Orthodoxy, the middle ground between the Haredi and secular poles. I'm far more concerned about the deteriorating relations between the various Jewish offshoots in my country. I'm afraid that if we don't ensure an inclusive and sustainable Jewish dialogue, this Jewish ship will head straight to demographic doom.

Years ago, in the States, I worked on a project dealing with conversion to Judaism, and interviewed rabbinic leaders from across the religious spectrum. I realized then that Judaism was headed for murky waters. Not only could community leaders and rabbis not agree on determining criteria for conversion, they couldn't even meet to discuss their differences. One Conservative rabbi stated that while he was "saddened" that Orthodox rabbis didn't acknowledge Conservative conversions, he couldn't, in good conscience, accept those of Reform or Reconstructionist streams. No denomination accepted another's definition of 'who is a Jew?'

The question is: how watered down can a denomination get before it is no longer identifiable as Jewish? Is it still preferable to be affiliated to any denomination rather than to none, or to be Jewish by halachic DNA alone? While the jury is still out on this, another debate is raging in Israel: the religious/secular conflagration, and the role of Zionism. It's problematic for me that some secular Jews embrace Zionism while entirely discarding Judaism. I don't understand it. How can a Jew forget he has a soul designed to follow a Jewish blueprint?

Secular Jews, overly reactive to Haredi manipulation on the national scene, have tragically rewritten Israel's script and dismissed aspects of Jewish life they view as inconvenient, archaic or distasteful. Here nearly every Jewish movement asserts that *it* is 'authentic Judaism.' In 'sophisticated' Israel, fashion, politics, and intellectual trends represent more than mere 'change,' they represent 'advancement,' and 'enlightenment.' Many Israelis don't even pretend to acknowledge Torah wisdom. They consider being a light unto the nations in a technological sense alone. Yet, our technologically vibrant nation, without ties to its founding Torah-centered wisdom, is on a shortcut to Jewish assimilation, if not annihilation. Being part of the technological rat race without a clear mission statement leaves one scrambling through the maze with no end goal.

Fortunately for Jews, the maze called life comes with explicit directions. A thoughtful examination of Jewish history, or a yearning to pass on the Jewish torch to future generations, should lead our nation to realize that Zionism without historic reflection will have no lasting momentum.

Pam, I fail to see how the 'Start-Up Nation' can come up with a Jewish contingency plan for future generations when it ignores its Jewish past. As a people, we have traveled this road before. The impulse to veer in a different, 'enlightened' direction, void of religious constraints, has been squashed repeatedly in the past. That's the deal our Maker has made with his Jewish charges. We, His nation, can embrace His plan for us, or discard it. We cannot, it seems, re-write His script on our own terms.

Recently my Zionist, religious cousin visited the States, where she noticed many of her Jewish friends were not only considering intermarriage, but actively seeking it. She lamented her grandparents' contemporaries discussing prospective non-Jewish grandchildren as a *fait accompli*. The failure to feel even remotely disturbed by this historical aberration, made her want to yell: "Great, another grandchild I can never date!"

I share her pain. I don't want the children of secular Jews to melt into obscurity. I want my own children to get the chance to know them, even to date them – as Jews. I'm on challenging yet familiar terrain here. Sandwiched between my secular sister and Haredi-Rabbi brother, I'm used to performing acrobatics when 'keeping the family peace.' I'm inspired by the words of Rabbi Samson Raphael Hirsch, a noted Torah scholar. He wrote about Jacob's final blessings to his children:

> "The nation that is to descend from {Jacob} is to be, in its external relations, a single unit..., a United Congregation of many types of people and professions. Each tribe is to represent a special type of person. The people of Jacob, as Israel, are to reveal to the world the directive power of God... not to show themselves as being in any way one-sided, but, as a model nation, shall present in a nutshell the most varied appearance of all different characteristics. In its tribes, martial nations as well as merchant ones, agricultural nations as well as scientific and scholarly ones... are all to be represented... it is to be made clear to the world that the devotion and sanctification of human life in the bond with God through His law is not dependent on, or conditional to, any special calling in life or national characteristic, but that the whole of mankind, with all its diversity, is called on to accept the one common conception of God, as taught by Israel, as so from all the different individual and national characteristics of mankind into one United Kingdom of God."*

* (Genesis 35:11–12, Isaac Levy, trans. Judaica Press, 1971)

Wow! Right on the mark, Rabbi.

Pam and Danit, we have a lofty ambition. Can we, Women of the Book, bring together disparate segments of Israeli society to celebrate the joy of being Jewish together, in this land of ours? Can we begin with ourselves?

Danit writes:

LOVE THE LATTES

I wouldn't know where to begin fathoming how I ended up a fully-fledged member of the Haredi community, but here I am, almost twenty years later. If you knew me before I became observant, you would understand the incongruity of me living in the Haredi community. This says more about the Haredi community than about me. Yes, I made adjustments, difficult ones; but the community accepts me as an individual looking for the path to Truth. I stepped into the Haredi community in Israel as a ferocious individualist, wanting to be guided. The good news, that may surprise you, ladies, is that I was not asked to become anything else; merely to change certain behaviors.

Picture flying red hair, tight blue jeans and a spirit to match, and you will see a young woman who could have ended up in India, barefoot on the vast beaches, painting gestural watercolors and writing poetry. Instead, reality presents a woman barefoot indeed, but pregnant and in the kitchen, for the past twenty-plus years. She is now the mother of nine and grandmother to the cutest-grandson-you-ever-did-see. My choice to live within the confines of the 'ultra orthodox' is a classic oxymoron. I was raised on nude beaches of California where banners proclaimed 'make love, not war.' I grew up on a diet of atheistic philosophies claiming 'dogma is man's worst enemy.' My world was one of bean bags, psychedelic colors, and being 'cool.' Today I find myself amongst men who dare not look at women in the eyes, and women who dress in formless tents.

You will ask me whether I belong here. My answer is a resounding YES.

"How so?" you ask.

Good question.

I realize that this particular community is shrouded in mystery and myth. It is a community which pro-actively hides its essence, not wishing to be probed or understood, and I admire its total disdain for public approval. It has a 'frankly-my-dear-I-don't-give-a-damn' approach. This is true liberation. In contrast to striving to be avant-garde and on the cutting edge of whatever, I am now quite comfortable living quietly in my personal space, my *daled amot,* and not proving anything to anybody but G-d. To be part of a community which vilifies the material and glorifies the spiritual feels truly cool, as opposed to another empty promise puffed out in smoke. The Haredi community is determined to do what is right without consulting image experts.

What the community lacks in PR, it makes up for in soul-searching. A community, not unlike a person, has an expertise which can exclude other facets. A person whose language is empirical and digital, can't always speak his feelings, an artist negotiating spiritual spheres may spend all day looking for his keys. The Haredi community's expertise is precise adherence to the letter of the law. Members stringently and zealously maintain the status quo of the written and oral word.

That comes with a price: unpopularity.

No one likes the diligent kid with the thick glasses in the corner, showing up the rest of the class. However, every class needs one. We are the nation of the book; the Haredim take that literally. They have never learned how to present themselves to 'outsiders' – not in Ashkenaz, nor in Public Relations 101 classes in universities.

Their men have funny looking things growing from behind their ears (including my sons, from childhood on), and beards; always the beards. The women are covered down to their eyebrows and up to their necks even on the hottest days, no tank-tops here. Women sit at the back of the bus, reminiscent of some of America's 'separate but equal' decrees. The religious rationale eschews interpretation by outsiders. Our explanation is simple: by law men are forbidden to shave certain parts of the facial hair, women must not be treated as public property, and intermingling of sexes, even on a bus, is asking for trouble. Women don't make a point of looking 'unattractive' – rather they try to avoid appearing sexy. No one wants to exclude women from buses or public venues; they must just be separate from the men.

Israel needs a community which upholds the structure of Jewish law. To have a peephole into the Haredi community you must accept that its centerpiece is the G-d piece. You may not want a peephole; you may not care to know. Fine. But then don't besmirch the Haredi name by judging them on their external appearance alone.

If we ladies truly want three-way communication, we need to delve past the external membrane, the persona; past the fabric of inner workings and into the essence: the original idea and life force of community. If we are stuck on how things appear and feel, we will be driven by heart strings or nerve strings with no connection to objective truth.

All communities are a validation of life style and choices. As a newly married woman, I personally never wanted any community. A free spirit, I would not subjugate myself to an artificial set of mores just to please Big Brother. In my suburb adjacent to Beverly Hills, eight kids ago, I had no problem parking my car and opening the door directly to my kitchen, without seeing a soul. I never needed sugar or flour from the neighbors; I didn't know or care about the Feinstein divorce.

However, having been raised to think independently, there comes a time where old theories no longer work. Real life begged me to change.

Pick a reason to join a community: children, friends, recipes, assistance in your hour of need, partners in your joys. There are so many perks, including eye contact with a like-minded, friendly face. My Dad used to say that man can live as an island, never needing another soul. I disagree. When I became observant, Dad wondered what I did with his daughter and from what planet this imposter had landed. Most importantly, when would the real Danit be back? Little did he know what was yet to unfold. He was the classic wandering Jew; we never stayed in any country for more than a year. His free spirit kept him running, running away from stability.

There are many things I would not have been able to share with my Dad, had he been alive today: the last minute dash to the neighbors for baking soda or eggs, the huge lasagna at your door when a friend hears of your bed-rest while pregnant with twins, the desperate rush across the street to the experienced mother who has married off many children, for parents-in-law advice – all this is a real net under your tightrope. When three heavily pregnant friends sat around the *Lag Ba'Omer* bonfire fantasizing about our offsprings' future games of cops and robbers (which panned out exactly as planned), we enjoyed the pure synchrony of it. When 'Auntie Helen' was sick with age, my oldest fed her soup. I am not sure who the giver was and who the receiver.

In the States, I pulled down the nudes I had painted, and put up the Rabbis. I threw away the jeans, and put on a scarf. In Israel, the stringencies are much stricter. Here I am asked to sit at weddings apart from my husband, minimize contact with external culture (movies and internet), and to patronize only institutions which are *shomer Shabbat.* Despite my keen sense of self, I never felt these expectations infringed on who I am. They simply ushered me along on my odyssey.

The Haredi community recognizes the innermost being, not the materialistic part of the person, or the 'feel good' part. It does not necessarily cater to the ambitious change-the-world piece. It is custom-made for the super-cerebral or 'conscience component' of someone who is asked to refrain from the bad, and to do the good (*Sur Mi'ra Ve'ase Tov.*) The community asks the individual to work from the inside out, rather than be influenced by the outer.

I buy my ticket to this exclusive group daily. Yes, it is expensive, and it keeps me aware of my obligations and the purpose of life. I am buying strong borders, a clear code of behaviors. There are no questions about what is/isn't accepted. The groundwork is extremely stable and based on systems that have worked from time immemorial. The Haredi community freezes time from an innocent, naive place where men and women were separated, parents knew better, and Rabbis commanded respect. In this frozen time and space, technology hadn't yet enslaved us, and fads and fashion were not obligatory.

Others may see us as an anthropological remnant of ancient Judaism, and occasionally take their children to 'look at the nice Haredim, see how they dress, talk, sway...' However, we are a living, breathing entity which is not going away. Why? Because we have a strength that is not accessible to the outside world. On all levels, this community has proven to be the healthiest lifestyle in Israel, and the most enduring.

Chapter Two

Why We Love Israel

Pam writes:

ISRAEL AND ME

Call me boring, call me dumb: my basic line on where and how I want to live my life has not changed since I was ten. I was born in 1957; on the third day of the Six Day War I came home and announced to my parents that I was going to live in Israel. I suggested they join me. We lived in South Africa at the time, in a small city by the sea with shining, pristine beaches that stretched for miles and miles and more miles. The water in our ocean was friendly and warm, our multiple maids made sure that our home was as sparkling as our pool, our food was spectacular and plentiful and never cooked by us; Agnes, our live-in chef did it all.

I hated South Africa.

At age ten, bombarded at *Habonim* with raw footage from the still recent Holocaust, and stunned by the news of the war broadcast continuously over transistor radios placed strategically in corridors and classrooms at school, I begged my parents to leave our paradise-in-exile. Over dinners of rump steaks and lamb, with garden peas and oily oven-roasted potatoes that hit the taste buds with a thump of delight, I *nudged* and nagged. "Why can't we live in Israel?" I whined. "After two thousand years we have the chance to be a free people in our country...and we choose to pass it up? Are we mad?"

"Israel," said my dad, as he chomped on his chop. "They're fighting wars there. It's not a good place for a nice Jewish girl. Pass the salad, please."

At fifteen I proclaimed that I would go alone, to Jerusalem, to study English. At sixteen my parents started to crack, and scheduled a family holiday to the Holy Land, so I could see the campus and the dorms, and change my mind.

I didn't.

At seventeen I stuffed Cadbury chocolate between my new floral sheets and fluffy towels, and jammed jars of Nescafé into my boots. I slipped an iron, a hairdryer, and a complete set of cutlery into a coat bag, which I carried on the plane in the pre–security days, when parents walked up to the steps on the tarmac for a last tearful kiss. I left South Africa on a gorgeous January morning, and landed in Lod on a bleak winter's eve; but I was home. I was a baby, loaded down with so much luggage that I couldn't see over my trolley, but I was home, and help was at hand. A sweet oldish man (Jewish! Everyone was Jewish!!) helped me with my cart, and I gratefully surrendered all my worldly belongings. He pushed, and I floated alongside, through the throngs of shouting taxi-drivers (Jewish! Everyone was Jewish!!) and passengers and personnel (all, all Jewish too), until we found my cousin.

"Why did you take a porter?" he asked, by way of greeting. "Couldn't you manage your trolley alone?"

He tipped my Jewish grandfather, who, it turned out, hadn't really loved me on sight, despite my leaving three servants and a pool to come and join him in our own land. Never mind. The biting rain was Jewish rain, the honking drivers were my kinsmen, the sun that set at 3.35 p.m. was the sun that God gave to me.

I was home.

The next day my cousin went to work, and his wife went to work, and their kids went to school. I came down for breakfast – Jewish cottage cheese and sweet rolls, Jewish tomatoes and cucumbers thinly diced, coffee with milk from Jewish cows. Suddenly in the midst of all that Jewishness there was an almighty crack – a boom! Crash!! BANG!!! – which sounded decidedly Arab. I was seventeen and a long way from home; I knew someone was out to blow me up, back to where I belonged. I dived behind the couch, and there I stayed, shaking, till my cousin called to warn me of sonic booms from low flying planes.

Oh.

Over the years I have learnt much about drivers who honk, and things that go boom and shatter dreams and hopes and prayers. I have almost forgotten about cool rain that splatters and splashes on a hot summer day, washing away the heaviness. I've stopped comparing the beaches of Tel Aviv to those on the Garden Route, and I can eat Elite Chocolate without grimacing. I don't gasp with pleasure at a bus driver in a *kippa*, or shiver with astonishment that my kids call me "*Ima*." Israel has become home, not merely 'home.' My parents followed me here, eventually, and are buried next to each other in the town where I live. My brothers followed too, and served in the army; one lives close by; our kids laugh together in Hebrew on Friday nights and *chagim*.

And, after all these years, a flag flying from a car window on *Yom Ha'atzma'ut* still gives me that 'Hatikva Moment' – a thrill of joy from being where I want to be. A 'Shabbat Shalom' from the supermarket cashier makes me smile with the heart-leaping loveliness of living right where it all feels right.

And, when the strains of "*Ki MiTzion Teitsei Torah*" drift across our garden fence from our neighborhood *Beit Knesset*, as I float with my family in our Jewish, plastic pool, in the muggy sunshine of another Middle Eastern Day, I say a silent prayer of thanks for the dreams of a ten-year-old that are still coming true.

Danit writes:

THE ROCK OF ISRAEL

I could wander the world with a backpack, or drift from Europe to the Americas, only because I knew I had a home base. Waking up in Scotland as an eight-year-old girl ('geerl', as the natives say) or in Holland at eighteen with a map of attractions in Amsterdam, I did not feel detached. It was fine to visit strange lands, (and even live in them), as long as there was Israel.

Ever since I remember, I have been totally in love with Israel. My childhood summer trips were the highlight of the year. The Nimrod sandals, silly kibbutz hats, beaches, the sun, treks in the desert – all felt like mother welcoming me home. Still on the plane, I imagined landing into her not-so-full bosom, to be hugged and welcomed very warmly in the summer heat.

As I grew, so did my love for Israel. The fun and games blew away with the winds, but something else stayed. Israel seeped into my being beyond summers on the beach, beyond a philosophical truth. My senses soaked up Israel. The smell of pine in Haifa, or fish in the Jerusalem *shuk*, or salt in the Dead Sea, made me heady with pleasure. Even today the sounds of taxi drivers yelling juicy instructions make my heart skip a beat with love, *ahhh*, Israel. Israel has a certain color, personalized and specific. It's mute and soft, something ochre. It tastes hot and spicy, like falafel. It's not *vivid*, it's *Israel.*

As a woman nesting and bearing children, it was the promise of home that drew me here. Landing in Israel was coming home, where I belong. I felt like a fish finally sliding into his pool, which quakes with pleasure to welcome him back into the velvety waters.

Israel is not beautiful, or lush, or grand. She never promises riches, security, or serenity. At times she's loud and overbearing. She can demand and be fussy. She's not always stable, and rarely relaxed; with so many personalities she sometimes seems schizophrenic.

I choose Israel not because 'it's worth it,' or for the offer of something I can't refuse. I choose Israel because, like the love of my life, there is no other. There are no other pools for this fish. She's the only one. This is not an infatuation that passes the morning after. It's true love, for better or worse. I'm here and here I brought my children, to share that love and belongingness. I brought them home to mother's embrace.

After years of introspection, my husband and I gave up the expensive brick walls in Beverly Hills, the pool in the back yard, the maid, and two excellent cars. I'd just buried my father in the exile of Los Angeles and wanted no more promises of riches and jet-set success. Both my husband and I were wandering Jews in the spiritual and physical sense; ready to bring our children home, even at great material cost. No more living 'the good life,' no more philosophizing about Israeli politics. It was time for the real thing.

I flew alone with sixteen boxes, four little children, a fifth on the way, and a good dose of determination. My husband stayed behind to finalize business affairs. At the other end of that trip I found myself, in the middle of the night, in a cold, dark, broken down structure pretending to be a house in Ra'anana, with four exhausted children and no electricity. As I bent down (with difficulty, due to the swelling belly) to pick up my crying toddler, I let my purse fall off my shoulder and whispered "we are finally home." I was the same age as my mother had been when we left Israel over thirty years before; my oldest was the same age I had been then: eight.

It didn't take me long to realize *home sweet home* came with a price. The thing I love *and* hate about Israelis is their frankness. I walked down the streets and received free advice: my baby was cold, hot, hungry, fat or thin. At the bank I got a lecture on how to be a woman in my own right and not trust my husband with all the banking. The first time I went to the supermarket, I stood and waited for the checker to bag the produce. She sat too, waiting for me to do the same. The exasperation was mutual. *Ahhh*, Israel.

I quickly learned the ropes, and became an authentic Israeli. More difficult was – and still is – to be a Haredi Israeli. I'm still working on that. I brought my children home to practice the Torah of Israel, in the Land of Israel, as a people of Israel. That not everybody agrees with me is a no-brainer. It's the hatred of the 'other' that shocks me. The 'melting pot' mentality I absorbed in America still rings true for me. American Jews are very different from Israeli Jews, and that itself is a culture shock.

Sixteen years later, I still love Israel and my brethren – the Israelis. We all breathe the same air. Sibling rivalry is a sad fact. I may be a strange apparition in some parts of Israel, covered from head to toe in the heat of the summer and leading a flock of 'ducklings,' but nonetheless I feel at home. Funny, isn't it? In Beverly Hills I was never hated but felt like a stranger in a strange land, whereas in Israel what I sometimes feel, feels like hatred. It comes from missing information about each other. Yet, though the strife is unfortunate, it is not on a core level. Deep down we know we all belong here.

Our history reveals an amazing people. Ever since the Exodus from Egypt, a disproportionate number of us have strayed from 'home.' In Egypt, we were buried in the Plague of Darkness. In Greece, we became Hellenists; in Spain, Marranos; in America we are assimilating into the greater community. Throughout the generations we have always lost huge numbers of family due to historical circumstances. Those who still identify with the Jewish People are few, but strong.

We have astounding tenacity and a will to live. We are survivors;

perhaps that's what makes us so headstrong. The Jewish Nation lives! The smaller we become, the louder we are. We could be so much more effective in our small piece of the world, our home, by being united. *Shalom* always comes in the wake of war. '*Shalom*' means different pieces fitting together to make a much bigger whole. I still believe Israel is 'The Great Mother' making a home for all, and may the rest of her children come home quickly.

Tzippi writes:

TOUCHING HOLY LAND

There are dozens of people at the LAX terminal check-in counter. I make sure twenty-two suitcases, one husband, and five children are still intact. The El Al flight will depart for Israel in two hours. My mother is tenderly holding my eight-month-old son, kissing him every few seconds. She blows endless kisses to my other children, tears streaming down her face. It's all I can do to hold myself together. Two months of preparation for our big move to Israel have ill-prepared me for the moment of leave-taking from my parents, other family members, and perhaps of our very senses.

I turn to my husband.

"David, I'm not sure I want to do this. I can't. Look at my parents. We're breaking their hearts. This move is breaking my heart. What if something goes wrong? What if they take seriously ill? (They do – they pass away a mere year later.) I won't be able to live with myself." (It's hard.)

The day of our departure, Los Angeles gives us a gift: clear skies and beach weather. The kind of day when the whole family gathered to relax around a meal. My folks are right next to me, yet everyone's far from relaxed. We've had so many beautiful days and memories here. My family, I'm leaving my family behind. I *really* can't do this…

David acknowledges my cold feet, but remains resolute, inching up to the ticket counter. The lump in my throat is solidifying. My Israeli mother taps me on the shoulder and says, "Whatever happens, Tzippi, never speak badly of your new homeland. It's my homeland; it's a part of me. If you put her down, you're hurting me. Never forget that."

All too soon, I'm whisked away, high above the clouds, digesting my promise to my mother. I can't get my seatbelt right. I fidget in my chair. Magazines don't interest me. Instead, I list my apprehensions about returning to a land where I had spent the Six Day War in a Jerusalem bomb shelter on the Jordanian border.

I have few mental pictures from my early childhood years in Israel. One is of being without my parents as the wail of the war siren pierced our Jerusalem apartment, causing my four-year-old body to stiffen. It was June, 1967, and childhood sweat poured down my back, making my velvet dress itch. The siren, signaling the advent of the Six Day War, was loud and angry.

I remember small feet jumping off the couch as I grabbed my baby brother by the wrist.

"You're coming with me," I said, more matter-of-fact than frightened.

"You hold my hand, and I will hold the bananas," I told Jordan. I was all of four, and certain I would save us both from starvation and Arabs. The siren wailed high notes and low; it was scary.

"I'm glad I have bananas," I said. "Now we won't be hungry during the war."

"I want *Ima*," he cried.

I remember being very mad at him, as mad as the sound of the siren.

"Hurry, we'll miss the war," I snapped, dragging Jordan down four flights of stairs to our bomb shelter.

Such were my memories as I flew across Europe, bound for the Holy Land. Even as I harbored painful moments, I also resurrected some humorous ones. There was the day I brought my friend Sarit's grandfather to class for 'Show and Tell.' I was five and we lived in Haifa on Abbas Street, today an Arab neighborhood. Sarit lived close by and attended a different class. Every day we played together in the pre-school courtyard, and walked home side by side. One day, she announced she was bringing her grandfather to school; I told her to be nice and share – her *Sabba* should visit my classroom, too. She agreed, and the following morning, I walked into class hand-in-hand with Moshe Dayan, the famous general with the trademark eye-patch. I remember that my usually cranky teachers were rather solicitous of me that day.

Shortly after take-off and miles from L.A., I turned to look at my children seated behind me. Did I really just deprive them of a family-infused upbringing in America? As I poked at airplane food, I reflected that my children's futures were now bound up with a shared Jewish destiny, lived on a singular land. What the heck was I getting myself into? I was so torn.

Most Jews don't get the chance to live out their lives on the same turf as our forefathers Abraham, Isaac and Jacob inhabited. Most Jews don't gather up their convictions and merit passing them on to the next generation in their own land; most don't even contemplate being pioneers. So, why in the world was I signing up my family for this job?

To be sure, we humans know there is a deadline by which time our stories must be filed. But most of us don't consider filing our stories from Israel. We might give *Aliya* a passing, whimsical thought, which usually fades fast. But, just sometimes, we make a move to capture and continue the biblical narrative that we call our own. I remember Rabbi Pinchas Winston's words when I confessed my initial hesitation about uprooting us all and moving to Israel. "Peel yourself off America's walls, Tzippi, before G-d does it for you," he had said. Rabbi, you really knew how to make my day...

Eight years into our *hit-ya-shvut* (settling into our new homeland) the machinery of denial has failed. We did actually pack up the contents of our house and American lives and move here. It's not my imagination. Sometimes, I would rather that it was.

Has this move been easy?

No.

I close my eyes and remember our lives before The Big Move. I miss California, land of the blessedly tanned, gifted in climate and consumer convenience, abundant in educational institutions of great spectrum and opportunity... why would anyone leave? Add to that the heftier consideration of extended family, happily and firmly anchored to the golden turf, and one who threw caution to the wind and left the Golden Medina could be dubbed certifiable. And yet my family made the move.

Living the first year on trial membership on our *yishuv* landed us front row seats to a headline-making stage. We were actors more than spectators as we endeavored to write, negotiate, and filter our lives through Israeli lenses. On most days, apart from when I threaten to leave for one reason or another, we are playing our parts in an historic drama entitled: *The People Israel.* I know it will take time for us to feel at home. Stories take time to imprint, to evolve into a coherent narrative.

Eight years ago, as our plane descended toward Tel Aviv, a tiny matchbox plot of land called Israel beckoned to us. It beckoned from under a pile of political debris, a tangle of historic weeds, and discarded relics of Jewish emotions. It beckoned as the only piece of real estate in the entire world belonging to the Jews. It beckoned, and we came.

The question soon became not whether we would grow to fill the land, but whether we would allow the land to fill us. You don't come to Israel for the Zionism alone. You come in search of your Jewish home. They say that acquiring Israel is not without pain and tribulations. Building this country, this House of Israel, has its price, both figurative and literal. The process has torn at the foundations of the Jewish nation, taxed the strength of my people, and cemented our fates to this land. On a personal level, it has often been tough. Yet, for all of the angst, it has stopped us from being perpetual tourists in the world. Instead of tourist status, we get a sense of family.

I'm sitting in my backyard. The rocky cliff face framing the Ayalon Valley is a silvery silhouette on this sun-drenched land. On this day, my children are demonstrating their near-native language proficiency. They seem comfortable in their Israeli skins. Somehow my 'observer' status is melting away... snatched into this historic script, moving in a direction that I can't fully comprehend. *Home...*

Chapter Three

Cross-Dressing in Israeli Society: A Core Struggle with Sexuality, Nidda and Hair Covering

Danit writes:

EMPOWERMENT VS. SUBJUGATION

Many stations in my *Teshuva* odyssey were outstanding both in their difficulty and their reward. And always, the more difficult the change, the more rewarding the outcome. Modesty of dress was a 'doozie.' The transformation that was expected of me was almost a deal breaker. I crashed up against this early in my process; my 'baby' at the time was women's lib and freedom of dress. I held the flag up high and yelled: 'I'm a pro-choice woman and in your face!' I cheered those who threw out aprons, put on high heels, and knocked with gumption on equal opportunity doors. In contrast, this modesty station asked me to throw away my tight jeans and cover my elbows. Most difficult was to cover my hair (which took me years.) From where I was standing, I didn't understand the connection between elevated femininity and modesty in dress. I went kicking and screaming all the way into formless dresses and scarves. When I was ready, I took on a two-pronged process: to understand *why* I had to put a *shmatte* on my head, and to negotiate with G-d.

Tzippi was my wailing wall. To her, I bemoaned my struggle with hair covering. How to do it? Should I let out bangs? Allow a little pigtail to show? I finally gathered the courage to go to a lady selling scarves. She slapped a snood on my head and, with much flare, brought me a mirror.

The cloth was white and made me look like I was recovering from brain surgery. My spontaneous tears were hot and stung. The worst part was that she didn't understand me at all. She was flabbergasted. My tears were born of terror; I knew there was no way out. I was going to end up like her, wizened in her black snood. Maybe I would wear a beret, just on Shabbatot?

Meanwhile, Tzippi's lawyer husband walked by to refill his coffee, cocked his head towards us, (men love women's conversations), and blurted out, 'Just do it!' Notwithstanding the coffee he stretched out his hands, perplexed that I was still debating this, with my own hair exposed. I was stunned by the simplicity of his statement.

David was right; thankfully G-d is patient. I wanted to understand this thing called modesty first, before covering up. Well, that is a conundrum; you can't learn to swim by reading a book. First you must get wet.

The difficulty of hair covering doesn't render it unnecessary. Truth is not fluid; it can't vary with our state of mind or political views. An absolute Truth is an external point of perspective by which we measure ourselves, and according to which we change our behaviors. Therefore, I had to first cover up and then ask why.

The larger community approaches life from the opposite end of the spectrum from us. They say: first feel good, and then begin movements to support these feelings. It's tempting to stick an arrow in the middle of the tree, draw a circle around it and yell "BULL'S EYE!" especially when everybody's doing it. Something about my life felt less than genuine.

The process of *Teshuva* is a search for an unencumbered place, free of ambition and embarrassment, uncluttered by comparison and competition. It presumes a transformation of thought and deed. It strips away layers of comfort which deaden the life force; it allows real contact with the 'self.' The process demands change for good reason, and comes with tremendous enlightenment. It defines who I am as a woman.

I am a treasure beyond price, given the gift of beauty and grace, but only for eyes which appreciate the treat. I am a hidden treasure, to be discovered and unwrapped. Nothing about me is taken for granted. I live in quietude, knowing my place in the world is carved and fixed. I don't need to prove anything, or do anything, in order to be. I am, therefore

I am. I don't knock on any doors or allure my way into positions. The only thing I need to do is to know I am as G-d wants me to be: a treasure.

It's still excruciating to cover my hair.

G-d knows.

Once I finally arrived at the inevitable conclusion and covered my hair (long... red... curls... thick... shiny... and bouncy, sob!), I began feeling a remarkable change in people's behavior towards me. My statement was loud and clear: 'I am married and I wear that fact on my head for all to see. My covering is my crown of glory, a physical embodiment of a core value of Judaism – marriage. Marriage is sacred: untouchable, non-negotiable. I draw a line between me and the rest of the world. I am separated and protected by my status. A society without such borders is a chaotic one in which all is possible, dependent on whims of physical desires.

The extreme and difficult act of hiding my hair illuminated a hidden reality. I, as a woman, had effused sexuality. That was my G-d given tool. On an unconscious level I realized my tool early, and used it to advantage. This is a fact of life which all girls know, from the word 'GO.' The media relentlessly badgers us to change our hair color, smooth our skins, go on diet. We buy clothes that accentuate sexuality, and, best of all, we are told to reduce/enlarge our breasts. The media, the mouthpiece of society, yells relentlessly that without sex appeal a woman is nothing. She must fear fat, aging, stretch marks, and crows' feet. At first sign, she makes a beeline to plastic surgeons.

The Haredi dress-code speaks volumes of bad taste and self-effacement to the secular. Why be choked around the neck with a tent, why wear stockings above the knee, and formless skirts? Why not figure-hugging shirts and even pants? For heaven's sake, say the secular, ours is the era of freedom and unisex. Get with the program, you pitiful Haredi women. Show yourselves. You have nothing to be ashamed of (even if you had ten children before you were twenty, and your body is... well... changed.)

I say to them: the reason I cover my body is not because I am ashamed; I cover my body because I am proud. What is underneath the tent is my business only, and only I choose what to do with it. I am keenly aware of my sexuality, so much so that I choose to secure it in a contained environment where it can be used most potently, with elegance, rather than become a clumsy spectacle for all. It's like a desert flower, delicate yet fiercely alive, which needs a natural environment to survive; a woman's sexuality is endangered if not protected. However, in its natural environment – the bedroom – the *kodesh kedoshim* (sacred of the sacred), it becomes the origin of life, the glue between a woman and her husband, the nucleus of the home, which is the nucleus of Judaism. A woman's sexuality is G-d's greatest gift to mankind (I don't say this lightly), and must be treated with the utmost respect and care by men and women alike.

If we approach women's sexuality from the dark side, we will recognize its power by how it's been abused. Burning 'witches,' breaking little girls' toes, performing genital mutilation, and discussing whether or not a woman has a soul, are all side-effects of the fear in men's hearts. What do they fear? They fear the mysterious hold women's sexuality has on men. It is the one force men could not conquer throughout the centuries, and one which they never will defeat. It is a treasure enjoyed only by the appreciative heart. A heart not in the right place will be consumed by it.

Dare I play around flippantly with such power? Dare I wave an extremely sharp knife with which I cook a gourmet meal just to 'see what happens' in the name of freedom of spirit? If I display myself for men's edification, or play 'show me yours and I'll show you mine,' am I not ripping apart a desert flower? In the secular world my body sells cars and cigarettes! Women 'compare and contrast' their waist lines and vital statistics. Why should my body be in contest? It belongs to me. It is the only one I have. My mission is to use it to enjoy my sexuality, promulgate life, build a Jewish home, and hug my children.

My community understands this. We live by the halacha with precaution, because we see the extreme consequences of the alternative. We peek into the dark side of life to identify the enemy, and then set up borders accordingly. I believe in sharing values which others hold dear, but I know man-made values are easily negotiable when circumstances change. Haredim do not play with fire. The result is button-down shirts and socks.

Many women don't include their names on invitations to joyous occasions; they don't feel a need to advertise their positions. I was written down as my 'husband's wife' on our daughter's wedding invitations.

I was not consulted. While ideally I would have liked to print my name, I felt no anger or remorse. I know my place as the mother of the bride; my position was loud and clear, without the need to use my name.

The intense process that happens underground before a tiny piece of green grass finally forges through is no less important because it is not seen by the external world. The feminine essence sings out clearly from behind the scenes. Similarly, the most important moments in the Torah were intimate ones, unseen by the public. A Jewish home is the pinnacle of *kedusha*. It is where most mitzvot are performed, from Shabbat to *kashrut* to raising children. Because it is sacred, it is hidden from view. The Jewish home is not a public place. The Jewish woman is not a public figure.

It's a sad commentary on society when men don't get excited by women. When men are deadened, or tired, or desensitized to a woman's body (or hair), that is the beginning of the end of humankind as we know it. The magnetic attraction between man and woman is the nuclear axis on which the world spins. That is nature and that's the good news. But the attraction between the sexes is like a super-sensitive machine which needs a clear, directive manual for its upkeep. This machine is the throb of the community, the life-force. When we reveal what should be hidden, or hide what should be revealed (true femininity), the machine breaks down. Then marriage crumbles, and the very fabric of society begins to erode. Haredim are aware of this visceral, primal truth that the larger society has chosen to ignore, in the name of 'equal rights' or 'freedom.' Perhaps we live in a time of slavery to freedom? We are so enslaved to the idea of freedom that we forget true connection happens only within the borders of absolute Truth.

Every woman feels the power in her hair, her body language, in the inflection of her voice. Every woman knows her strength, and must be careful not to misuse it. We have been trained to use what we've got to survive; we've been told that the more sex appeal we have, the fitter we are in this jungle of life.

But is that really true? Or can we find our sex appeal with just one person who is more than enough? That place of grace is within the strict borders of marriage. Can you look at your man as the 'one and only?'

And now you have a gift to give him.

If you can really do that, all talk about self-expression through bikinis feels irrelevant. To speak or not to speak into a microphone at my son's Bar Mitzva is not a question. Wearing T-shirts or button-down shirts will not matter.

Classic feminism was about allowing women to be more like men. Why did we poor women need a movement in the first place? Only underdogs need movements; the downtrodden, untouchables. Am I so incapable of looking out for myself that I need a movement? Apparently, yes. This movement said: "you can be equal to a man. We will do you a big favor and treat you like men."

Thanks, but no thanks.

Torah's approach is true feminism. Torah teaches that a man without a woman is considered dead. She is the source of blessing, joy, and his home. The woman breathes life into him and keeps him honest. She is his authenticity, his measuring stick. She was created to bring him down a peg and remind him that he is no god, but simply another creation.

A month after we made Aliya, I decided to cover my hair only when I left the house. My two-year-old was picked up for preschool at seven forty-five, not a time when I was about to go anywhere, so I had no hair covering. I would kiss her from behind the door and send her off to join the other sweeties in the car. The driver was also the Rabbi of the school, which meant I couldn't play around. He was a typical red head; when he came up our driveway he had no time to waste. One fateful day, he honked from around the corner. My baby toddled down the paved path. The Rabbi's energy whirled around my baby's feet; she lost her footing and fell flat on her face. She wailed in pain and humiliation, the car was honking and I was behind the door... with no head covering.

That was the turning point. As I ran to comfort my baby, I was uncomfortably aware of my uncovered hair. I felt humiliated and torn. Obviously I needed to go to my child, but I felt naked in front of the rabbi. There my dilemma ended.

Tzippi, tell your husband: I just did it. From then on I always covered my hair.

Pam writes:

CROSS-DRESSING: CULTURAL, CULTISH, OR JUST PLAIN COMFORTABLE?

I constantly cross-dress. Every morning I pull on my jeans as I grab a cup of coffee; at night I slip into my husband's T-shirt to sleep. Like millions of women who regularly transgress the Deuteronomy dress-code*, the reason is purely pragmatic. Jeans are comfortable. Men's T-shirts are soft and cheap. Power doesn't come into the equation; our generation's gender struggles have moved beyond clothes. Only recently a regulation was passed in New York entitling transgender citizens to Birth Certificates stating the gender of their choice, irrespective of biological make-up. When a woman who is physically a man can be registered as having been born female, cross-dressing does not scream significance.

Yet the casual attitude of the new millennium towards cross-dressing is by no means universal. Men still don't wear mini-skirts, unless they are traditional-and-trendy Scots. In certain circles trousers for women are still taboo. Amish women wear modest dresses or skirts, exclusively. Hassidic women do not cross-dress. Among devout Muslims, swathing the body completely threatens to become de rigueur. At Bar Ilan University, where I researched gender and clothes, cross-dressing by female faculty members is frowned upon. Nearly five hundred years after Shakespeare dissected the impact of clothes on the gender-war, the same anxieties are still contentious, contemporary, and compelling.

Equally compelling as in earlier eras is the place of women in our high-tech, high-maintenance, high-stress world. Men and women may mostly dress alike, but cutting edge cognitive theories suggest that their brain capacities might not be that similar. Just ask Larry Summers.** On this hinges the whole skirt/trousers/should-I-show-my-elbow debate. *It*

---

* Deut. 22:5 "The woman shall not wear that which pertaineth unto a man, neither shall a man put on a woman's garment: for all that do so are abomination unto the LORD thy God."

** Recently Larry Summers, the then President of Harvard University, ignited the academic world by asserting that women's brains are not as geared towards Math and Physics as their male counterparts. Summers has since left his position at Harvard.

has nothing to do with sex or lust or causing some poor weak male to lose concentration for holy texts as his eyes wander to a woman's knees. It is men clinging onto their power to rule the world, to run the woman into the ground, to literally and metaphorically wear the pants. And all power to them, if women are wimpy enough to allow this.

Oh Tzippi! You claim, below, that "real feminism is being lived more in the modern orthodox circles of Israel than along the streets of Tel Aviv. If the goal is to not objectify women as sex objects and instead to emphasize the internality of women – then religious Jews have something to teach fans of Steinem and Friedan. Our slogan could very well be: 'Say no to provocative – say yes to radiating quality.'"

Radiating quality? I look around at harried, overweight, old-before-their-time religious women sweating in long dresses and long sleeves and long wigs and I don't see any quality except that of exhaustion ... just as men would want. Exhausted women are too tired to demand more rights; especially if they are working too, to support their men's yeshiva-habit. Their men can trip home on Fridays and sing "*Eshet Chayil*" to demurely-dressed wives, who have chopped the salads and set the *Shabbos* clocks and cleaned the house and bathed the many babies, and who probably flop into bed too tired to enjoy the pleasures of Friday night sex.

Ah, sex! Here we come to the crunch of the matter. Sex, sex, sex. Why is sex such a terrifying concept to the religious world? What the —— (I could insert an appropriate four-letter word, but I won't) is so awful about sex? Yet this total preoccupation with the evils of sex has less than nothing to do with clothes. The passionate belief that jeans, or t-shirts or bikinis lead to mass rape or worse, is just anathema to me. In her seminal, life-changing book, *Infidel,* Ayaan Hirsi Ali, a Muslim turned atheist, describes how young girls in her society are taught that a host of angels perch on their shoulders, to ensure the pure of heart don't show an ankle, God forbid, or an uncovered head. When Ali fled to a Dutch refugee center she was horrified to see women in skimpy swim-suits chatting to men at the swimming pool. She was sure it was the end-of-the-world; she feared vicious, out-of-control men would ravage the almost naked girls. Imagine her surprise when these same men spoke politely to their sexy companions, and treated them with respect. More respect, Ali realized, than she had ever witnessed Muslim men giving heavily swathed Muslim women who do not taunt with a naked elbow or knee. *How women dress has nothing to do with how we are treated by men.*

Tzippi! You yourself admit questioning your abrogation of 'normative' clothes. "Do I feel less feminine?" you ask, (below), and answer, "No, not really. I remember feeling less feminine at times when I used to wear pants." *So what is the problem then with pants??* They seem to you not so alluring after all to sex-mad men, who need just a curl of hair to think: SEX, SEX, SEX.

Ahh, jeans and hair. Alice Shalvi, winner of the Israel Prize, founder of the Israel Women's Network and long-time headmistress of Jerusalem's Pelech Religious Girls' High School, is the daughter of an Orthodox Rabbi and a devout Jewess herself. She wears trousers, and doesn't cover her head. "The Deuteronomy prohibition is for a woman not to wear man's clothes," she explains, "and I never wear men's trousers." Clothes have evolved since the Bible was written – ancient Hebrew shepherds probably wore something like skirts. Shalvi claims that proscribed hair is disheveled hair; tangles make men think of you rising from bed. "My hair is always neat," she maintains, "I don't need to hide it."

Oh dear, oh dear, oh dear. If hair is a woman's crowning glory, and wives must cover up except in the presence of their husbands (and lords?) alone, why can young unmarried women flit around with hair blowing seductively in the faces of poor pure male scholars, who are forbidden to stroke it? I don't understand. You say hair is so sexy that it has to be covered from *Chuppa* to grave. So why is hair free to shine in the morning sun before marriage, but single sexy shoulder blades are banned? What the hell's the difference? And why can married women wear glorious, shiny, silly wigs, more sexy by far than their often mousy hair?

I read Danit's chapter and despair. Really I do. Maybe the men I mix with, (who don't ever study *Gemara*), are different from Haredi males. I have to say, truly, in all my fifty-five years of life, I have never felt like 'a piece of meat with eyes,' as Danit told me in conversation she feels when she dressed in tight jeans. Jeez, do you *really* believe this stuff?

And why, oh why, oh why are we so worried about sex? I think sex is great; I'd hate my girls to be hung-up and make it into *such a big issue*. Whew. In our *kodesh kedoshim* sex is also the glue between my husband and me, and our gift to each other. Yet I go outdoors with uncovered hair. And so does he.

If you told me that in the religious world no-one had intimate relations until their wedding night (or even thought about the pleasures of being wrapped in someone's strong/tender arms . . . in silky sheets . . . stop! Stop! Danger!! EEEeeeeeekkkkk . . .), and thereafter sexual congress was trouble-free and spiritual forever, and both parties thought of higher things and making babies in praise of the Lord while doing the business – if you told me that with your hand on your heart, maybe I'd change my mind. I believe, however, that the total opposite is true.

I believe that in the very devout world the poor yeshiva *bochers* have sex on their minds, *ve'od eich*. These kids, who turn into men (who do not go to the army) spend hour upon hour cooped up in study halls poring over the minutiae of Solomon's seven hundred concubines (or was it two thousand?), and how King David saw Batsheva brushing her long hair (the *naked* Batsheva, it has to be added), and how to check your wife's level of purity after her menses by stuffing a white cloth deep inside her – you get the picture. Then there's Judah, who mistook his daughter-in-law for a prostitute, made her pregnant and abrogated responsibility . . . that's before we mention ole' Onan, who didn't sleep with his fantasy so spilt his seed on the floor. *Years* the yeshiva boykies study this stuff – and a short hemline would be too much for them?

C'mon.

Don't tell me that there are no sexual issues in that world – and that demure dressing leads to happy-ever-after marriages and spirituality in the home. I don't believe it for a nanosecond. I'm convinced the Haredi world is more concerned with sex than the normative world, on balance, or at least just as much. This making it all so forbidden, so dangerous, so huge is just so very sad to me. I'm sure it's why Haredi boys burn dumpsters so often – they need some avenue of escape. But that's another chapter.

Dressing demurely is one big hoax. It's the equivalent of Chinese women binding their feet and cracking their bones so that they could not stride strongly through life, next to their men. It's the equivalent of female circumcision that makes women ache, and weak, and unable to hold the reins of life. It's the equivalent of the *niqab* – what's the difference? – and Amish flowing skirts – and it's a male plot to keep women down. No, Danit, men throughout the ages and in every religion haven't feared women's sexuality, they've feared their power. Looking like a wimp, covered from head to toe, turns you into one. (*Nothing* to do with sexuality. Women in long silky wigs look more sexy than those having a bad hair day.)

That women buy into this nonsense is the strangest thing.

Here's another thing: the crux of the sex-gender controversy (are women intrinsically weaker than men or do men manage to make them believe that they are?) has always hinged on two disparate yet complementary issues: the perceived essential difference between men and women, and their commensurate status in society. Academics, thinkers, and anthropologists all weigh in on the question. Thomas Laqueur, for example, (Professor of History and American Sexologist), states the obvious: the "oppositions and contrasts" between the sexes have been self-evident since the beginning of time: "the one gives birth and the other does not, to state the obvious".*

Yet questions about gender have gripped men and women ever since there have been men and women; and they transcend the observably biological and physical variations. Discounting the 'otherness' underneath their clothes, were men and women *innately* different, wondered philosophers, or merely culturally programmed to fulfill antithetical functions? The debate spilt over into the realms of morality, religion and cultural mores and norms: if women were not equal cognitively or emotionally to men, did that mean they were inferior? Was a woman's place, as the theologians argued, subservient to the man's? What were her rights in the family set-up? And, of paramount importance, how threatening were signs of female excellence to men? The answer hinged on one's stance: are women innately different from men, or do they only function differently in society because of cultural conditioning?

Since early modern times, clothes – or more specifically: who wears

* Laqueur, Thomas. "Orgasm, Generation, and the Politics of the Reproductive Body." *Representations* 14 (1986): p.3.

the trousers – has been a central pillar of the debate. In the thriving Elizabethan England of five hundred years ago, puritanical ideas gained ground in a vitriolic clash with the vibrant theatrical world. On the streets of London ladies' fashion came to embody contemporary questions of gender, power and the status of women; a trend that was mirrored on the stage. Cross-dressing was a primary site of dissension. On the one hand it provoked religious righteous anger at the women who broke the 'Deuteronomic Dress Code' and paraded publicly "in that which pertaineth to a man" despite Divine censure of this 'abomination unto the Lord' (Deut. 22:5). But cross-dressing not only displayed a scandalous disrespect for God through the proscribed appropriation of man's clothes, it also signified, to outraged puritan spectators at least, a direct threat to man's dominant position in society. Phillip Stubbes, one of the most outspoken of the Puritan social reformers, proclaims:

> Our apparel was given us as a signe distinctive to discern betwixt sex and sex, *&* therefore one to weare the Apparel of another sex, is to participate with the same, and to adulterate the veritie of his owne kinde. (Sig. F5v)

Cross-dressing could emasculate husbands, and turn their wives into power-hungry 'men-women,' eager to wrest control. I claim that religious men of today are not different – Jewish, Muslim and fundamentalist Christians alike – they keep women covered from head to toe, and thus safely out of positions of power. And women from all the religious streams – Jewish, Muslim and Christians alike – largely lap it up! They willingly tuck their hair under scarves or berets or hats or wigs, and swaddle their bodies under *jallabiyas* or shapeless skirts or long sleeves – and they say they feel better for it!

Go figure.

From: Danit Shemesh (danit.sh@spidimail.co.il)
To: Pam Peled (pam-peled@bettaletter.com)
CC: Tzippi Sha-ked (tzippi@connectisra.co.il)

Yes, Pam, of course the boys (and girls) learn about David and Batsheva, Yehuda and Tamar, Ruth and Boaz, and the Garden of Eden and much more. Yes, they sit on their *yoshev* and learn about sex. The yeshiva is the place to learn about it, in a kosher setting, where mothers and fathers know and trust the messenger, as opposed to learning on the streets. We are not ashamed of sex; we don't hide the fact that *David HaMelech* was active. We simply channel the subject correctly, teach it in a supervised setting, and make it age-appropriate. We learn what is allowed and what is not through our heroes, who also made mistakes. Our heroes are examples of positive and negative behaviors. We have no saints in our religion, thank G-d. Traditionally mothers taught girls about sex, and fathers taught boys. Isn't that wonderful? That tradition has died away; there is no time for children anymore, send them off to 'professionals.' Pam, your scorn comes from not seeing the big picture; it comes from twisting and collapsing things into a tiny perspective so they fit your 'opinion.' That is at best unscientific, and at worst discriminating.

Tzippi writes:

> *"If I had to characterize one quality as the genius of feminist thought, culture, and action, it would be the connectivity."*
>
> – Robin Morgan
> (American radical feminist-activist, writer, poet and editor of *Sisterhood is Powerful*)*

GO SEE

Cape Town, South Africa, 1983:

"The mini skirt is an accessory to your smile," says my manager at Mulligan's Modeling Agency. The 'smiling' wasn't as much a problem as was the idea behind the VIP party to which I was invited at a very posh penthouse in Cape Town. Modeling scouts from New York would be checking out local goods. "Dress in black, hike up the skirt, smile and walk the runway while our guests sip cocktails" was my directive.

That night, with a rebellious hemline inches below the dress

* Lewis, Jone Johnson. "Robin Morgan Quotes." About Women's History. http://womenshistory.about.com/od/quotes/a/robin_morgan.htm. Retrieved: April 2013

requirement, and a foreboding view of the Twelve Apostles, I lined up with four other models to strut the makeshift runway. The room was crowded with black-suited American VIPs, alcoholic beverages, and one reluctant model. The fast beat music hijacked our senses and pulsated in eardrums; the 'local goods' stood ready. I watched the first model use her mini-skirt as an accessory to her winning looks. The 'professional' all male scouts looked her over in a decidedly 'unprofessional' manner. My nausea set in, making the room spin. Pearly white smiles melted into hemlines, alcoholic vapors interfaced with American accents, and the flash of cameras lit up the South African night. The room spun faster. This was not an acid trip, but rather a case of buyer's remorse. I left the penthouse before the second girl had completed her run-way walk. And I never returned to modeling.

What was my 'threat alert' at that moment? As I left the who's who of the Ford modeling world, I felt an intense loneliness. I was being scrutinized up and down but no one saw me for who I was – a caring person, a good daughter, an author, a television show host. What they saw was another nameless model in a sea of women with short black hemlines and made-up faces. Worse than being marketed by my agency, I was marketing myself. I was in extreme danger of being rendered invisible, and aiding my own disappearance. And what for? Recognition as a model? A fat pay check?

A storm was brewing across the horizon, in sync with my shifting line of vision. Attending an all-American public high school in California ensured that my beauty barometer came from central headquarters: Hollywood. Fully made-up face? Check. Heels? Check. Cute outfit? Check. Swagger? Check. Cute guy? Check-mate. Hollywood appeal is not relegated only to the schoolyards of Southern California. It has infiltrated most of the western world. Even Israel, a full-blown democracy, the spiritual epicenter of monotheism with concomitant ethical conduct, has bowed down to fashion idols. Even Babylonian gods would wince!

A clothing chain in California called *Ross* boasts: '*Dress for Less.*' I now appreciate the unintentional meaning of that advertisement. It's possible to not only dress for less, but also to be viewed as less, a veritable two-for-one sale! A lovely secular cousin of mine dresses her pretty young daughters in low-cut tank tops and closely-cropped shorts.

When I point out that guys will ogle them, she counters that this is less about fashion than about weather in our furnace-like country. She later admits that while her own twelve-year-old is different, most of her daughter's friends have boyfriends. In nurturing her daughters' homage to weather, and encouraging dressing for comfort alone, might she not be encouraging a direct correlation between attire and pre-pubescent male attention?

How confusing for kids to be slaves to fashion, the weather, and parental expectations, while forging their own sense of style. My twelve-year-old cousin insists girls dress for boys. "Isn't that a pity?" I ask. Her mother reprimands me for making the girl uncomfortable and says that her family has different values from mine. I hadn't meant to offend, even as her child paraded in front of mine, in her tank top, in our religious neighborhood. This mother obviously placed greater value on personal comfort than on respecting religious sensitivities. But, hey, it was only my home and my neighborhood. After all, it's a free country.

With all this freedom comes a price. I have a sinking suspicion that fashion dictators have robbed children of childhood. My little cousins are sexually objectified, and exposed to pernicious behavior from boys their age. When do they get the chance to build themselves as young ladies? When do they assert their rights as innocent children?

With respect to Gloria Steinem and Betty Friedan, true feminism is being lived more in the modern orthodox circles of Israel than along the streets of Tel Aviv. If the goal is to not objectify women as sex objects, but to emphasize the internality of women, then religious Jews have something to teach fans of modern feminists.

During my very brief modeling days, I remember sipping a cold drink outside the agency between 'go-sees' (modeling interviews.) At the next table a tall, handsome male model poured over a book. I looked over my list of instructions: to greet the designer with a genuine smile, and arrive early so photographers see me with fresh eyes.

I laughed out loud, inadvertently attracting the attention of the reader at the next table. He looked at me expectantly, and I shared the irony in the term 'go-see.' This was hardly a place where anyone could be 'seen.' I noted the 'genuine' smile – what was remotely genuine about being looked over like a hunk of meat, even with 'fresh eyes?'

Gila Manolson sums this feeling up:

> "But if I know who I am, who cares how others see me? No matter how much we think we know who we are, our sense of self is greatly impacted by our interactions. The resulting self-image could be called the "looking-glass self," formed by others' impressions of us. In short: "I am who I think you think I am" – how others see me is how I come to see myself. If so, it's crucial that our interactions strengthen who we really are."*

While modeling, I struggled with the notion that I was 'dressing to impress;' in search of outward, not inward success, and for a pay check. So, I reverted to my Modern Orthodox sensibilities and toned down the 'form' to reveal more of the 'substance.' Dressing now involved representing my outer self as a reflection of my 'inner' make-up.

Manolson puts it: "*We all want to be visible. For some, being visible means being noticed. For others it means truly being seen.*"** My own revolutionary process meant dressing for self-empowerment. Noting how some young girls dress quite depressed me. They seem sexualized at younger and younger ages. What are parents thinking when they send eight-year-olds to play with midriffs hanging out and half a *tush* showing? Parents are inconceivably enabling a value system that eradicates adult/child behavioral norms – even before their daughters' braces are off!

Pam you write: "*Ah, sex! Here we come to the crunch of the matter. Sex, sex, sex. Why is sex such a terrifying concept to the religious world*?"

That's funny, Pam. In Judaism sex is good and holy, and *even required!* But sex is also about context. Sadly, for some young ladies, there seem to be no boundaries. Just about any place or time is okay for sex, as long as there is 'love' – or is that also passé? Sex has become the social currency, or insinuations and innuendos to that effect.

As I started dressing Modern Orthodoxish, I aligned myself with a certain uniform. Was this any different than donning the uniform that

---

* Manolson, G. *Choosing to Love: Building a Deep Relationship with the Right Person – and with Yourself.* New York: Distributed by Feldheim, 2010. p. 70.
** Ibid. p.73

my job required? The funny thing about dressing more conservatively is that I became more aware of how others viewed me. Did my uniform align me with a movement that tries to reflect its value system and priorities? Yes. Was it uncomfortable? Yes, at times. It can be bloody hot wearing longer sleeves on a sweltering day. Does Jewish law demand that my attire set me apart from society in general, and discourage me from aligning myself with the sexual norms and mores of society-at-large? Of course. That is the bottom line, halachically speaking.

You have a number of arguments with the religious dress code, Pam. Here's one: Women should dress for comfort. If it feels good – just do it.

This makes perfect sense. Yet, by removing G-d from this equation, there is no wiggle room for Him as arbitrator of fashion limits. Ultimately, Pam, a bikini is just a bikini and, as you say, it should not lead to rape. However, clothing, by Jewish design, is meant to elevate the human condition, not bring it down to the animalistic level. So, a bikini might be appropriate for some at the beach, but not at a family outing in the mall. Religious Jews want to raise the level of societal standards for everyone's benefit.

Religious women also strive for connectivity. True feminism, Jewish style, fosters a potent, attractive sense of sisterhood, unleashing spiritual energies that men can only dream of. Competitive and conniving behaviors exhibited by girls and women vying for eye-candy status under the tutelage of fashionista squads is notably absent within the religious arena. Religious women have more important things to keep them occupied. The beauty and fashion contest has been replaced with feminine camaraderie and a disassociation from society's more vacuous trends. Take a listen to Melinda Reist:

> "Raunch culture has taken us back. It's an absolute tragedy," "[Women's] liberation has now come to be seen as the ability to wrap your legs around a pole, or flash your breasts in public, or send a sexual image of yourself to your boyfriend so he can pass it around to his mates. Girls think that empowerment lies in their ability to be hot and sexy."*

---

* Melinda Tankart Reist, founder of Collective Shout, a group targeting

Modern Orthodox gals shouldn't have to sacrifice their attractiveness. Do I have the same lenses/perspective as my Haredi sisters? No, not really. Sorry, Danit. That's one of many reasons why I chose the Modern Orthodox milieu. While, in some ways, our dance is hard for you to understand, it's also more nuanced, negotiated, discerning, and rewarding. We combine the thirst for secular and religious knowledge with halachic sensitivities. We travel in many circles, distinctively, but not as strangers. Our modest attire gets the job done without attracting negative attention. Halacha, does not prevent me from dressing attractively. It does, however, hold me accountable to myself and to uplifting society in general. And, yes, this is an enormous responsibility. The point is, Pam, I don't see enough introspection or onus in secular quarters to elicit a higher code of fashion conduct and elevate society.

I am all for the empowerment of women (depending on its definition.) When secular people look at me, what do they really see? A Taliban poster girl? Do they take me seriously? Am I 'interesting?' Am I trendy, or someone who identifies with a group of women who accentuate different aspects of their being? You might argue that dressing sexily does not preclude being accomplished, and being taken seriously. Keep believing.

Pam, you are appalled at all the *racy* subject matters yeshiva *bochers* are learning. You write: "*I believe that in the very devout world the poor yeshiva bochers have sex on their minds, ve'od eich.*" Pam, religious Jews are not too prudish to talk about sex. However, the whole subject is taught very, very differently in yeshivas from the way it's presented in secular schools. The latter teaches the science, mechanics, and consequences of this human drive. The former elevates this drive, while discussing sex in the context of relationships among biblical heroes – the psychological, emotional, and spiritual components of these relationships, and not only the act itself. Maybe some Haredi men do get off on this and frequent prostitutes as you often cite, in spite of the context imparted to them via the Bible. I believe they remain the exception, Pam.

So are we going to have a meeting of true minds? Can I get Pam

---

companies that use overly sexual images of girls. From New Zealand Herald, *Feminist: Sex culture setting women back,* Simon Collins. Aug. 2nd, 2010.

to agree that secular Israeli women should work towards elevating the currently non-existent public discourse on public attire? Can I get Danit to recognize that Haredi women's dress codes may inhibit their outward elegance and draw negative attention?

Israel is rife with secular paranoia of the religious agenda. But let's turn the tables for a minute. Does a secular lifestyle enhance feminine power, or diminish it? Does it help or hinder young boys to see the intrinsic worth of young girls, and to seek a viable and lasting marriage partner? Are secular women more or less likely to find themselves competing with men for empowerment?

I don't believe that secular society contains nothing of substance. When it comes to dress, however, their mantra is definitely '*Less is More*.' These days, the accessory to more skin can only be a smile... for what else is left?

From: Danit Shemesh (danit.sh@spidimail.co.il)
To: Pam Peled (pam-peled@bettaletter.com)
CC: Tzippi Sha-ked (tzippi@connectisra.co.il)

Hi Pam,

I thought of you today, Friday. I remember saying TGIF every Friday morning as I luxuriously stretched out my day before a night on the town. Today I slave over a hot stove and bend over a filthy floor with my staff of hard-working girls, all of whom I trained well from age zero.

We whip up an amazing meal including fresh baked *challah* and all sorts of cakes from fruit to chocolate to meringue. Then we make salads, and chop celery, carrots, and tomatoes before moving on to the festive meat and chicken. We make three meals for at least fifteen people; us and a friend or two. The house is cleaned and shines. Each of us has a job in our well-oiled machine, and the entire household teems with life. Is it exhausting? Well, that depends on how you look at it.

If it's just the body lifting and peeling and bending, I suppose it is tiring even though healthy. If it's the *nefesh* we're talking about, that also depends on attitude. Am I thinking the entire time, "oof, why am I the sucker who has to do this just because I was born female?" or "How lucky to have this family whom I love beyond words, who are eager to eat what

I make. It is a mark of our bond and is rewarded with togetherness." We sit and discuss current events, tell inspiring *Torah* tales, enjoy each other's company on an existential level which leads nowhere but to enjoyment of a connection. We sing songs of gratitude and love for our Creator and are uplifted by the experience which becomes not the weekend but the week-center.

Am I exhausted after candle-lighting? I am too elevated by the anticipation of our 'us' to feel the body's *krechztens*. You may respond 'c'mon!' but that does not change the authenticity of my words. I am not saying you don't have this experience, but I am sharing mine with you.

Chapter Four

Keeping the Faith

Pam writes:

GOD

God and I are going through a rough patch in our relationship right now. A month ago my beloved, wonderful, kind, generous, good, gorgeous, helpful, handsome husband was diagnosed with pancreatic cancer. He is 62. This is not our first brush with this cruel disease. My beloved, wonderful, kind, generous, good, gorgeous, helpful, handsome father, who never smoked, died of lung cancer at the age of 61. My beloved, wonderful, kind, generous, good, gorgeous, helpful, lovely mother died of pancreatic cancer a few weeks after she turned 70; my best friend, the beautiful daughter of a Holocaust survivor, died of cancer when she was 45. I nursed them all.

My husband is in a different category: my parents and Julia were given no hope of recovery. With Martin we do have hope; and we are researching as hard as we can to find a way to help him regain his strength and get better*. So that's, I suppose, where God fits in now. Hundreds of people are praying to Him to heal my husband; even the Muslim women in my college literature classes informed me that they prayed to their God during the holiest time of their year, when the heavens are open to beseeching from below. My religious friends are praying for him, their kids have their Yeshivot praying, and our non-religious friends have found, to their surprise, that they are praying too. I am also praying to God, and to my parents up in heaven, to intercede for

* Martin Peled died shortly before this book was published. He was 64 years old.

us with God. And, please, please God, when Martin gets better I will thank God a million times.

But this is problematic, no? Is God the reason my exceptionally wonderful husband got sick? Why did our caring, truly pious, totally observant Rabbi lose his son of four in a Californian traffic accident, and then lose his young, religious, lovely wife to cancer? Why are the wards and corridors of Tel Hashomer full of kippa wearing, head-covered religious patients, who worship God three times a day? Clearly obeying His will does not guarantee health or prosperity; many evil individuals live well, to a ripe old age.

Why do we thank God when things go well, but not blame Him when they don't? I can't work it out.

I see, I really do, that it helps to believe. A sigh, a shake of the head, a teardrop trickling down a cheek with an 'it's all from above, it's God's will' eases the agony of loss if you have perfect faith that everything is for a reason. It's the old Holocaust conundrum – can there be a God who condoned that? Where was He? The answer: the ways of the Divine are mysterious; it's not for mere mortals to ask why. The questions are searching, deep and anguished; answers are necessarily pat and not profound.

And although it's profoundly difficult for me to focus on anything outside Tel Hashomer's Oncology Ward and the confines of our healing home at this point, in fairness to my relationship with God I know that I have to go further than my own pain to truly explore our connection. I believe in God. I believe in some power watching over the Jews, keeping us safe some of the time, keeping us on earth for so many centuries. I believe in the Torah, in the stories, in the rituals. I like lighting Shabbat candles, I like it when my husband sings "*Eshet Chayil*" to me, I like it that we wash our hands and keep quiet (mostly) until we bless and taste sweet *challah* on Friday nights. I like keeping kosher, at least symbolically. I love *chagim*. And I feel God's presence when we sit in our *Succa* with friends and family, giving thanks for our happy lives.

However, I think that God has been kidnapped in Israel. God, or those that speak in His name, are doing a disservice to our holy land. I would go further: in my opinion zealous religion is a direct existential threat to our country. Today is a good example: as I sit here typing in the center of Israel, vast tracts of the Carmel forest region are burning. Rabbi Ovadia Yosef, the revered spiritual head of hundreds of thousands of religious extremists, and head of the Shas party's Council of Torah Sages, pronounced on Saturday night that fires only happen in places where Shabbat is desecrated. Yosef ignored the many times Hanukka candles burn down religious homes, or that *succot* incinerate their orthodox inhabitants every few years when Shabbat candles flare out of control.

This ranting makes me want to head for the nearest pork and cheese burger and beg my girls to marry out of the faith. Rabbis rush to blame train catastrophes on insufficient Sabbath observance; driving on Shabbat was the 'reason' for the helicopter disaster during the Lebanon war. God has been hijacked by black-coated hysterical Haredim who hurl dirty diapers and burn garbage dumps when they feel His name is being abused – by building a bomb-proof emergency ward in Ashkelon, for example, on the site of where they contend ancient bones might be buried. It makes me sick. It makes me fear for the country. It makes me not want to be Jewish.

My God is a kindly God, who possibly wants a few – a tiny few – of his people to stick by the rules and regulations that He may or may not have dictated to Moses on the mount. They set the standard – standards that are not meant for the masses. I think God hopes that His people will not eat pork, just to remember they are different, and will fast on Yom Kippur, and know how to pray. But I really, really, really don't think God wants competitive *kashrut*, and different standards of *hashgacha,* and that He stands with a stopwatch watching who waits six hours or three between meat and a nice cup of tea.

No! No! NO!

I once read about how Hari Krishna initiates are welcomed into the fold. First they are told to count everything they see. Leaves on trees. Cars on the road. Fingers on your hand. Books on the table. Windows on the wall. One two three four five six seven. Over and over again. For days. By the time they're finished their brains are so addled that they'll do anything, believe anything. *Yeshivot* employ similar tactics. Study study study from morning to night, with breaks for prayer and time to recite *Tehillim* – scramble brains enough and they'll believe that God is great and God is good and God wants us to beat up those who write on Saturdays. When He is not busy burning their forests.

And if God says the pious should not go to the army, well, who am I to object? And if He says they should study all day so that their houses, at least, are safe – well, that's the way it has to be. And if God says Jew should lift up hand against Jew and fight against the (unholy) upholders of (unholy) law and order, hitting police officers without compunction... well, why not?

God is a dangerous weapon. More wars have been fought in His name than we care to remember – when did God bring peace to earth? I would suggest that He is left out of politics, left out of State, left out of schools. God is between me and my God; no-one has the right to tell me what I should/should not believe. If lost souls turn to God instead of to drugs or wandering the world, that's fine for them. But don't let them holier than thou me, or my country. Let them live in my country, and pay their dues – go to the army, work for a living, hand over their taxes and be productive. In their homes they are welcome to wait twelve hours between a kosher steak burger and a *badatz* milkshake. Just don't tell me that I should do the same.

And, while we're talking of God, please, please God, make my husband well again – fast. Please, please, please, please God.

Danit writes:

HA-SHEM

Who is anyone, really? Are you so-and-so's mother, sister? Are you someone's wife? Are you your profession, your age, your gender? Are you your bank account, your age group, your social status? Are you your star-sign, your personality? Or are all these things mere adjectives, descriptions that don't begin to say who you truly are? If you ask me who I am I answer: I'm Danit, an Israeli/American, born in 1962 (the hippie generation.) I am a mother of nine and a wife of twenty-five years to a wonderful man whom I admire. I am the daughter of a scientist and an artist, and sister to a psychiatrist. Do you know who I am now? The answer is a resounding no!

I have learned over the years that having a relationship with G-d is having a relationship with me. At the very end of my life, after I have discovered that I am not only my body, my emotions, my opinions, my experiences in life, my relationships; after I exhaust who am I, I identify a new, quiet voice, and that is G-d Himself. That is the *Zelem Elokim*, or soul, which breathes inside us, and wakes us in the morning. It is our desire, our inspiration, our purity, our goodness.

When a person dies he still has eyes, but they no longer see. That proves it's not the eyes that see, but rather the soul. It's the soul that lives and loves throughout one's lifetime. The *neshama* is the piece of us that's inspired, passionate, and loving. Having access to the G-d piece inside me, and having a relationship with G-d, is what propels me. I believe that I am a creation, loved by my Creator, not an accident dating back to apes or the Big Bang. My Creator created me for a reason. I'm not parenthetical or happenstance. G-d is not up there wondering 'Oops, how did *she* happen? What do I do with *that* one?'

G-d created man. Not the other way around.

I used to believe that man created god. Why? Man created god because he was too weak to deal with life. So he took on a belief system as a balm for open wounds. Belief takes the sting away. If there is a god, we can sleep well with wars raging, sickness ravaging, poverty striking…

I still believe that: man created god. That god is not the G-d with whom I have developed a relationship.

G-d is not the Wizard of Oz, a magician you trek down a yellow brick road to reach. He is not some box within which we deposit our provisions, checking off each item as we go about our lives: health, check; money, check; good kids, check; good relationship with hubby, check. Wait, wait, I forgot – getting into this particular school, check; or this particular soccer team, check. That type of relationship is human and conditional. The person on the other end is forever passing or failing tests. If you don't deliver the contents on my list, our relationship will be in danger. I have placed you (god), up there, where I need you, so I can be slightly less agitated about the unknown. If I continue to feel agitated, then what is your purpose? I may have to replace you. I may have to think of another way to feel less agitated. Perhaps a strong army will help, or an honest prime minister, or a good consumer report, or grass, or health food, or theories and how-to systems, or alternative medicine, or a guru. I will do anything not to feel the pain of life or the dread of the unknown. Opium for the masses, Marx called it. A man-made god does, indeed, keep the natives quiet.

Down here, in the land of The Tree of Knowledge of good and evil, all we know is relativism, confusion, and chaos. Down here, the 'peace' sign of England is the 'up yours!' of Japan. Down here, when I say 'I love you mom,' she may react, 'OK, how much do you need?' Down here, a fat woman is considered beautiful in Arab countries and ugly in France; white skin is preferred in Japan but in California, uchghgh, get a tan! Down here, we hold onto 'isms' as a lifeline in the insecurity of relativity. We don't have a formula for life. We look for the secret to happiness or stability and stick to people till they let us down. Down here, an innocent man can be arrested and a guilty man set free.

Down here, in the darkness, there are no answers. Truth is elusive. There are no quick fixes, promises or potions. We are on this ride and can't get off. Hope comes only from embracing the Absolute. This Absolute renders time and space transitory. It means acknowledging an Entity, as opposed to the concept of relativity. This Entity ensures that justice is not a fluid concept, but a hard and fast law. There's a reason for everything and anything that we cannot explain. There's a method to the madness that we cannot fathom, because *we* are relative beings. We are only a small piece of a grand puzzle. We believe we can see clearly from one pole to the other of this global village, but we don't realize this is just the tip of the iceberg. This world is nothing but a corridor to an absolute state of being where there will be no death, no sickness, and no relativity.

A relationship with G-d includes a relationship with nature and a journey into its laws. Jewish Law, Halacha, is a deep understanding of nature. Halacha, derived from the word 'to walk,' teaches one to walk in the way of G-d. It is *His* manual, the 'how to appreciate' what *He* created. It is a constitution, a contract; not unlike a marriage-contract. There are rules to everything in life.

Similarly, a relationship with G-d has foundational rules. You learn your own menstrual cycle to keep the laws of '*nidda*.' You observe exact time to know when to pray, when the sun comes up and sets. You explore the constitution of fabrics because of '*shaatnez*,' and the engineering of toys and clocks to abide by Shabbat laws. Are the contraptions automated or on spring?

Before you visit mourners, you learn psychology to enable you to act sensitively. Thus, you don't greet the mourner, unless he greets you first. Speaking may feel invasive. You can't touch him unless he requests it. Touch may feel like sandpaper against his soft underbelly.

You learn about animals and how not to mistreat them. Touching a new born kitten is forbidden; once touched by a human hand, the mother cat will not feed it. Feed animals before you feed yourself.

You learn not to be wasteful. Give leftover food from weddings to the poor.

Laws govern everything. Laws of behavior forbid speaking evil about anybody, or embarrassing people in public. You may not remind a convert that he is a convert and you must invite guests to your home when they have no place to go. You may not look into people's windows, nor surreptitiously listen in on their conversations. This is called stealing their consciousness (*'gezel daat'*.)

Social hierarchy is clear. When a teacher or Rabbi enters a room, you stand. Never contradict your father; you may disagree without forgetting who he is.

These laws and many, many more teach us that every move we make in this world counts. We have the power to destroy as well as to build; the rules and regulations remind us that our choices are meaningful.

I once heard a Rabbi recount an email. It went something like this:

> I understand you were looking for me, that you sent me countless letters that I didn't return. I am terribly sorry. Your question is why the Haredi people need to be so particular and picky. Why can't they simply live and let live? What difference does it make if they light candles one minute later or earlier?
>
> By the way, the reason I couldn't write back is that I never got your message; you forgot the dot before the com.
>
> Yours truly…

After five years of intense learning about halacha and precise behaviors, I decided to add to my curriculum. Following the letter of the law to the T was not satisfying; I wanted more. Like I expect more from my husband: more intimacy, more communication, more mutual understanding – I am a sort of emotional perfectionist – I wanted more from my relationship with Judaism. Halacha became the vehicle, the framework for everything else.

I looked at my own reality and realized it was custom-made for me. There were no mistakes. I accepted it not out of submissiveness, but from a place of choice; it is the path G-d chose for me. It helps me reach my purpose in life most accurately and efficiently.

If I were intellectually honest, I would admit that I have made few choices in my life. I did not choose the parents I was born to, or the places where we lived. Although it seems a choice, marrying my husband was more of a force of nature. It was a light-bulb moment where I plugged into my divinely ordained destiny. The different layers of me argued non-stop until the highest layer won out, and I married him. I did not choose the children I had, or the people I would meet. I 'chose' my occupation by virtue of my talents, which I did not choose. I barely chose the place I live, it was a financial choice made for us.

So where *is* choice? It is in *how* you live the life you are given. It is the dignity you find in any situation. It is about perspective and translation. That's what having a relationship with G-d means: accepting and loving the reality He chose for me and believing it is best for me. It means accepting your body, your age, your bank account, your children just as they are, and your husband. If you had the choice of vanilla or vanilla, which would you take? *Of course* vanilla, and you may even enjoy it. We, as Haredi people, believe in the ultimate shepherd who leads us perfectly. We are not lost sheep fending for ourselves. We have a leader and our connection to him breathes life into us moment by moment. The choice is how to live that life, and the choice I made was to become Haredi. As Chazal say: "Everything is in the hands of *shomayim* (heavens) with the exception of *yiras shomayim* (my awe of the heavens.)"

The human spirit can fathom both bad and G-d. The human spirit is fascinating and admirable. Each person is an amazing being who keeps on going through fire and ice, to live and make a statement. That is who we are and that is the indication of our relationship with G-d. The human spirit lives on forever, well after our death. Our spirit chooses how to live, and love, and be inspired. What we do with our lives is what we leave for the next generation. G-d is not an additional thing, another ingredient in the soup of life. He is life itself. He is my inspiration, my reason for being. He defines me.

G-d asks me every day, are you still with me? Are you sure?

Up to now, the answer is still 'Yes.' Not always standing upright, sometimes on my knees with exhaustion, but I'm still here.

Tzippi writes:

> *"Your mind works very simply: you are either trying to find out what are God's laws in order to follow them; or you are trying to outsmart Him".*
>
> – Martin H. Fischer*

GOT G-D?

I read a lot of books about G-d; those written or inspired in His name and those denying or appropriating his message. I even read books that use G-d in the title as a marketing tool. You can call me a G-d book hoarder, on permanent Google alert for G-d. In my house, it's blasphemous to say G-d is left on the shelf.

I scan the most salient titles: *The Reason for God,* Timothy Keller; *A History of God*, Karen Armstrong; *The Secret Life of God*, Rabbi David Aaron; *Between God and Man*, Abraham Heschel; *The Way of God*, Moshe Luzzatto; *God is not One* by Stephen Prothero; *God is Not Great*, Christopher Hitchens... the list goes on. My bookshelves groan under celestial weight. On a lower shelf are two more: *Doubt: a history,* Jennifer Michael Hecht, and *Who Wrote the Bible?* by Richard Friedman.

When did this thirst for knowledge of our creator first surface?

Raised in a modern religious household in Los Angeles, I attended secular public schools. I never even met another religious girl my age until high school. Still, thoughts about our maker arose out of nowhere, on a daily basis. By sixteen, I was a self-described religious existentialist.

While some friends half-heartedly pondered the questions of life: Why are we here, what is our purpose? – I was determined to find

* Matte, Gregg. *Finding God's Will.* Ventura California: Regal Books, 2010.

answers. Where to begin? After high school, I joined a religious girls' seminary and attended lectures on Jewish philosophy ad nauseum. I scoured libraries for books that could contribute to my understanding.

At university, I studied comparative Religious Studies – Buddhism, Hinduism, Islam. What does the human experience say about G-d? Tackling G-d, from both a religious and secular perspective, became an all-consuming passion. If there was a maker, I wanted to hear what he had to say. My behavior and raison d'être could not be dictated by me alone, I reasoned. Who was the highest authority?

While I did inherit a belief in a G-d together with my rich Jewish legacy, I had to fight my own battle for personal faith. Syrupy, '*touched-by-an-angel*' stories, from within my own faith and others', did very little for me. I was a product of my rationalist-scientist father and not going to 'believe' in G-d simply because my religion dictated it.

Either the cosmos was aware of my existence, or it didn't give a hoot, as there was no 'mind' at the matrix of our universe. All around me, the masses extolled 'reason alone,' precluding a belief in G-d. When there is no objective evidence for G-d's presence we are no more than random energies in time and space, with no ultimate design or guidance. This appalling world view is given a favorable spin by the staunchly secular and 'enlightened' (e.g. Christopher Hitchens.) The argument is that by dispensing with the ridiculous notion of a G-d, nonsense and superstition can be replaced with reason and moral progress – leading to the betterment of mankind. Love the math.

Here's the argument that is often cited, (by Pam too): "God is a dangerous weapon. More wars have been fought in His name than we care to remember – when did God bring peace to earth?"

As Dennis Prager ("Happiness is a Serious Problem" and "The Nine Questions asked about Judaism") counters: "The argument against religion that more people have been killed in the name of religion than by any other doctrine is false propaganda on behalf of secularism and Leftism."*

No question; religion is getting a bad rap. Yes, evil is committed in the name of religion and wars have been fought in G-d's name,

---

* DennisPrager.com, retrieved 25th May, 2010.

but statistically those casualties pale in comparison to atrocities committed in the name of Nazism and Communism. This doesn't justify religiously-inspired casualty lists, but does set the record straight.

I argue with my G-dless friends that placing one's faith in the wisdom of secular humanity to produce a moral utopia is pretty sad. Secular humanism has led us down a dismal road to a world of moral relativism. Even pinning grand hopes on 'democracy' as a vehicle for peace can backfire, sounding a death knell for moral reasoning.

As the English writer G.K. Chesterton says: "*When a Man stops believing in God, he doesn't then believe in nothing, he believes anything.*"*

My search for answers continued. My quest to pursue knowledge of a higher authority made me oppose any religious conviction with a pre-programmed, built-in resistance to anything not based on reason and science. After all, I was the daughter of a world-renowned physicist on cold fusion. But I also agreed with Pascal's wager: If G-d exists and you believe in him, you come out ahead. If there's no G-d, it doesn't matter either way. Believers have the bigger payoff. Still, I was not going to reduce my existence and its meaning to a coin toss.

My interest in religious studies clarified matters for me. "The Revelation of G-d," in the world's major and minor religions, often hinged on one man's revelation and *his* attempt to share it. The credibility of mainstream religions stands on the testimony of individuals: Buddha, Jesus, Mohammed, et al. With one exception: a 4,000-year-old text with a noteworthy claim: Three million people stood at a mountain called Sinai. Every man, woman and child present in the desert heard the voice of G-d. What a bodacious claim! There's no contesting notion or existing scriptural cannon that refutes this claim, so it made sense to begin my search with my inheritance: the Sinaitic text.

I rolled up my sleeves and dug through Jewish literature. Some days I woke up with blistering existentialist angst. Was any of this real? Maybe the Israelites simply mistook a 4,000-year-old hallucination for G-d? Is there any contrary evidence? If it never happened, was everything else so achingly purposeless? Other days I woke up a confirmed agnostic. I

---

* Cammaerts, E. *The Oracle of the Dog.* Whitefish, Montana: Kessinger Publishing, 2004. p .211.

couldn't prove that the Sinaitic experience didn't happen, so I considered the possibility that it did.

My search for answers became of paramount importance. Conversations with my father provided solace. My father was a rocket-scientist and renowned authority on metallurgy, cold fusion and rocket engines; my English name, in fact, is Faith after the Apollo. He attended an annual physicist convention in a different country each year, which he loved. He often told me how exciting it was to be in a room with the world's greatest minds. What struck him was how a disproportionate number of the world's top physicists – Hindu, Muslim, Jewish or Christian – believed in G-d. The more these scientists delved into the world of nano-particles and studied the substructures of the physical world, the more awed and convinced they were of a grand design and a thoughtful designer. On most days that fact quelled my rumbling search engine. If minds far greater than mine, with access to far more information than me, were convinced of G-d's existence, then I could hardly dismiss the notion of a Grand Being governing His creations.

Being a pragmatist, while studying Judaism I also studied Bible Criticism which claims that multiple authors wrote the *Torah*. Mulling it over, I realized that BC, though impressive, is tainted with an agenda to divest Scripture of G-d's authority. Also, it expediently fails to examine longstanding Jewish scholarship. My book shelves winced at the emotional burden of texts on Bible Criticism. Still, if I was to be intellectually honest and prove to myself the veracity of *Torah*, I had to contend with the critics.

To say that I grappled with G-d is an understatement. I never stopped questioning, challenging myself at every turn. We humans have a natural tendency to guard fragile positions in life, and not to be open to growth. I allowed myself to be open both to growth and doubt. Knowledge, like light, comes in waves and particles, it's not always linear. I determined to take a firm stance against society's mantra: Never let facts get in the way of your 'own' truth. Judaism is clearly different. One is responsible for one's own growth and understanding. It's not a religion that encourages complacency.

In time, my notion of G-d evolved. First my deity was simply a 'big brother' watching over me and judging, waiting for me to slip up. This

G-d was invented by my half-baked, childish rules. In my twenties, I only sanctioned a G-d that conformed to my comfort level; G-d forbid, my G-d demanded something difficult, sacrificial, or even inconvenient. Then I grappled with *Torah* texts, studied Jewish philosophy, and delved into comparative religious studies and I realized: the original matrix, the spiritual pump mechanism that empowers all forms of ethical monotheism, is Judaism. A news flash: G-d demands something of me as a Jewess. Whoa! As a Jewish wife and mother, I understood that G-d was a two-way street. Maimonides and Nahmanides say that G-d's relationship with us is based almost exclusively on how we relate to Him. I would not let society's norms hijack my G-d any more than I'd surrender to religious fanatics who hurt others in His name.

Pam writes that she fears for this country. *"(Fanaticism)... makes me not want to be Jewish. My God is a kindly God, who possibly wants a few – a tiny few – of his people to stick by all the rules and regulations that He may or may not have dictated to Moses on the mount. They set the standard – standards that are not meant for the masses."*

My *Torah* is different, Pam. It doesn't compute numbers of Jews who should ideally follow *His* rules. Nor does it state that these regulations are a mere celestial suggestion. My Torah was written for me and my children, for my community and my nation. If some misappropriate it and damage the intent, it's up to me to fight for its relevance. Despite Free Will, it isn't for me to opt out or re-phrase the Torah, but rather to preserve it and transmit its wisdom to my children. The traditional Jewish view of G-d doesn't absolve me of responsibility, or relegate it to others on my behalf. If the rules apply for one Jew, they apply for all. I have the choice to exercise the right and the privilege to call the Torah my own, while defending the right of others to ignore it and distance themselves from their heritage. I'll not run from my Jewish legacy, or hide when others appropriate our Torah to serve their purposes, nor will I shirk *halachot* that seem uncomfortable or irrelevant to others.

I grappled too hard to leave G-d on the shelf. No *doubt* there.

Chapter Five

Sex in the Small City

> *"Here's neither bush nor shrub, to bear off*
> *any weather at all, and another storm brewing;*
> *I hear it sing i' the wind: yond same black*
> *cloud, yond huge one, looks like a foul*
> *bombard that would shed his liquor. If it*
> *should thunder as it did before, I know not*
> *where to hide my head: yond same cloud cannot*
> *choose but fall by pailfuls. What have we*
> *here?"*
>
> – Trinculo, The Tempest, by William Shakespeare

Pam addressed a religious crowd in Tzippi's home and presented her book*: For the Love of God and Virgins* (*FLOGAV.*) The night proved memorable. Pam tackled issues like sexual slang in Shakespeare; not normally discussed in mixed company in religious *yishuvim*. A tempest in a coffee-mug turned into a veritable thunderstorm.

This chapter is devoted to the e-mails that followed Pam's talk:

From: Tzippi Sha-ked (tzippi@connectisra.co.il)
To: Pam Peled (pam-peled@bettaletter.com)
CC: Danit Shemesh (danit.sh@spidimail.co.il)

Dear Pam,

First of all, it was good seeing you and Martin, I was so happy that he could come. We enjoyed having you for dinner and thank you both for the gorgeous flowers.

There is some some feedback regarding the evening: most everyone that called felt you were informative, engaging and articulate. They had enjoyed the book and were looking forward to meeting you. Some wanted you to elaborate on the process of writing, the research, whether you were really 'you,' etc. Some wanted to hear more about how Shakespeare, the master of spin, connects to current events. Some asked about words that are 'spun' in the media.

But there was feedback of a different kind, which pertains to our project. Some felt they were cut from the conversation when it deviated in a different direction and that you lost an opportunity to promote dialogue with a religious audience by repeatedly referring to sex.

Pam, I very much appreciated your sensitivity in asking myself, my son Matan, and our cousin Rachel if it was appropriate to discuss sexual content during your talk. I remember responding "I wouldn't" and suggesting you stick to politics and to interesting aspects of hygiene etc. in Shakespeare. Matan and Rachel said the same. There is so much to talk about in your book: politics, international relations, the Shakespearean era, and characters.

As a friend, I was puzzled that you ignored our advice. While you were certainly a breath of fresh air, our *yishuv* wasn't quite ready for some of your content: repeated references to orgasms and ejaculations, among other things. Some of the audience questioned if I knew in advance you would mention sex so very often. I think it is important to know one's audience in politically and religiously-charged Israel, and perhaps respect their sensitivity.

True, you came across as engaging, knowledgeable, and entertaining. However, sexual references are not brought up in mixed company in religious circles. Religious Jews are not 'prudes' or uneducated; you had a very well-educated, tax-paying, IDF-participating and, yes, Torah-minded crowd.

It's respect for each other's beliefs, differences, and practices that led to our project: *Three Ladies, Three Lattes*. Did you miss the point? If at a micro-level we can address what divides *Klal Yisrael* by bringing three women from across the religious/political spectrum to present their positions and reach understanding and acceptance, perhaps we can encourage a *healthy* national discourse.

I guess this is a good time to come clean. I do have an agenda and it's not subtle. I want to build bridges. I want us to learn to co-exist before it's too late. It pains me to see Jews tear at each other. Perhaps we can showcase how much we have to offer without undermining one another's beliefs.

Back to FLOGAV and your talk. Your book contains an important political message. FLOGAV focuses on how the media can distort information about Israel. I'd like to see the same consideration towards Orthodox beliefs. How often do people read about Judaism from newspaper editorials that delegitimize it? All distortions are unfair. I think your book should be sold on American college campuses; despite your troubling, almost hateful stereotypes of religious Jews. Incidentally, the crowd at my home felt that FLOGAV would have been even stronger had you refrained from bashing Haredim.

I asked you to participate in *Three Ladies, Three Lattes* for two reasons: to work together on a dynamic, important project while exposing you to the 'other' (Haredim) in a meaningful, constructive way. For me it's about nation building, and seeing if Jewish internal relations can work. I suspect we may not be able to accomplish this. Sometimes I feel you now simply have a platform for anti-Haredi views. I fear we will not reach a resolution; rather we'll sense that *there is none.*

The challenge here, Pam, is to look for the light in the darkness, to look for redeeming qualities in Haredim that can launch a dialogue – a relationship even! Anyone can curse the darkness; the real work, the real creativity, the real *art* is to find a spark and let it grow. To merely denounce the darkness is *no accomplishment.*

The other day my daughter Ciona made my heart sing. She said: "It's easy to criticize others, but it's pointless unless you're willing to help that person as well." That is exactly what I have tried to teach my kids.

However, I'm not sure that we're on the same page at all with our project; it seemed a good idea until it got too personal. Danit's chapters make you groan. Your chapters, while engaging, simply emote instead of engaging with the 'other.' Your disdain of Haredim is so palpable.

Love,

Tzip

From: Pam Peled (pam-peled@bettaletter.com)
To: Tzippi Sha-ked (tzippi@connectisra.co.il)
CC: Danit Shemesh (danit.sh@spidimail.co.il)

Hi Tzippi,

Thanks so much for your email. I'd far rather talk about this in person, but if you prefer to discuss it electronically, that's fine too.

For me the Book Club was an eye-opener. Oh Tzippi! I am stunned at what some people perceived as 'sexual content.' One would think I stood in a bikini giving graphic details of pornographic, sizzling God knows what... where was the salaciousness in what I said? The only sexual reference was quoting Shakespeare – Shakespeare!!

I broached the subject after Chani (who bought a book!!) suggested I write an expunged version, so she could give it to her 19-year-old daughter, mother, and 92-year-old granny. My answer came to me when I was falling asleep – does she allow her daughter, and mom, and gran to read the Bible? King David, old and infirm, with a virgin in his bed – pedophilia, no? That's after he spies the naked Batsheva. Judah and Tamar? Amnon sleeping with his sister? Shlomo with 1000 mistresses? Noah all uncovered in his tent, and drunk to boot (with that hint of messing with his own daughters.) Quite racy stuff, no – is it allowed?

Tzip, you are one of the nicest, most special, caring, warmest people I have ever met – I came away from your house wishing you could be my Best Friend Forever. But the hysteria over what some people in your home call 'sex' has made me feel dreary, weary, and very, very sad.

You know what? I have lived in Israel for over 35 years – through wars, hyper-inflation, terrorism, and more. I have loved every day of living here, and never questioned my ideals. But this encounter makes me realize Israel is changing; what you call "the expectations of a religious audience" I fear is hysterical puritanicalism, and it's gaining ground. I don't want to live in a country which more and more resembles Iran. For the first time I feel I need to leave this stifling environment, fast! Isn't that sad.

I have much to say on this subject; it's pivotal to everything we hold dear. I felt this huge divide in our last chapter, and it cuts me to the heart; the gaping chasms between the super-'religious' way of thinking and mine, seem to be more and more insurmountable. Not sure where this leaves our book.

By the way: my professor on Milton at Bar Ilan U – a class that was full, full, full of literary allusions to sex – was Haredi, black coat, the lot. He had no prob talking about it in a mixed class. How come?

I'm sorry that you got flak from the evening. I think I won't talk at any more religious homes, that's the only solution I can see. I can't not talk about sex when discussing Shakespeare – how would I manage that?

It's very depressing to me. It has to be a hard way to go through life, so serious and holy all the time. Whew.

With lots of love,

Pam xxx

From: Danit Shemesh (danit.sh@spidimail.co.il)
To: Pam Peled (pam-peled@bettaletter.com)
CC: Tzippi Sha-ked (tzippi@connectisra.co.il)

Dear Pam,

I loved your book; it's a great way to showcase the Israel/Arab conflict, and the discrepancy between the appearance and reality of the conflict. I was looking forward to hearing you – it's always inspiring to hear artists speak.

So I kissed my babies goodnight and stepped into my carriage headed for Tzippi's inviting home. The crowd assembled and sat down on her plush couch and plastic chairs and the curtain came up.

At first, you seemed excited and a little flustered, but quickly you found your footing. You were here to share. I was curious about how you felt in front of a group of men sporting *kippot* and women with head coverings, who automatically separated themselves by gender, through ingrained social mores. I wondered if you noticed that, and what you thought about it.

Your love for your 'baby' oozed out and the book took center stage, intriguing everybody. You spoke of your editor's expectations and how your vision prevailed, and of your love for Israel. Your understanding of journalism was obvious.

Then there was a pause. Perhaps you thought you were boring us, or had exhausted your subject. Maybe you just couldn't resist pinching us to see if we 'live.'

You then explained why Shakespeare featured; you said you wanted to raise the level of the book. I didn't understand why, but who am I to argue? Then you described in detail Shakespeare's obsession (my word) with sex. You may have sensed the shifting in seats and whispering, as a definite response to your stimuli.

It was very interesting indeed, I must say (breathed Edith Bunker with hand clutched to the chest.) It was enlightening and embarrassing. Enlightening because Shakespeare was always a mystery to me, and on my 'wouldn't it be nice to understand' list and you gave me a tiny peephole into him. Embarrassing, because you were talking about things our community does not discuss in mixed company. We were all mature adults, yes, but you should have respected our communal mores. We don't take sex lightly, we don't banter about it, or joke about it, or try to understand how the neighbor is doing it. We, a group of mature, educated individuals, uphold the value that sex is intimate and should be treated intimately.

What perplexed me was your desire to teach me. I wanted to learn about your book; not that being a 'prude' was obsolete or primitive, or maybe even detrimental to my children. "Do you honestly believe that your mother never had sex?" you almost said to the woman who wanted a censored version.

I loved FLOGAV and was fascinated with Shakespeare's take on sex, but I couldn't understand the connection. What does Shakespeare have to do with politics? It felt forced: you love Shakespeare and you want to clear Israel's name in the eyes of the world; so you somehow merged the two.

You said you incorporated sex to sell the book, to make it more readable. Is that not underestimating your readers? Is it we who are prudes and clueless, or are your readers over-sexed? Can Shakespeare think of nothing else and thus writes it all cryptically – incognito – or do you not believe that the book's central message is enough?

I know, Pamela, that you have a lot to say to the world and I love the idea of free speech, but every good speaker needs to know his/her audience. You were in front of observant Jews, whom you are not about to 'educate.' Most of these people have thought long and hard about how they want to live their lives and what to sacrifice to stick to that plan. They make the sacrifices willingly and will not be swayed, because they reap the fruits of their efforts.

What is your main goal with our project? Are you using it as a forum to emote or do you really want to understand that the Nation of Israel includes us?

We come as we are, not pliable. Do you want to know us intimately, or to judge us from the outside? If you love Israel, as you say, which will be the better choice?

Yours,
Danit

From: Pam Peled (pam-peled@bettaletter.com)
To: Tzippi Sha-ked (tzippi@connectisra.co.il);
Danit Shemesh (danit.sh@spidimail.co.il)

Hi my ladies – got your letters, will respond soon.

Do you know what my Haredi friend from Jerusalem told me yesterday? He said a very learned Haredi said apropos *Yom Ha'atzma'ut* that "Israel is like a retarded child... it just sits there."

Did you see a Haredi newspaper expunged the picture of Hilary Clinton... but wait! This will be in my response... watch this space. Interesting it certainly is.

Let's all be well well well well well... in the end that's all that really counts.

With love and hugs, Pam x

From: Pam Peled (pam-peled@bettaletter.com)
To: Tzippi Sha-ked (tzippi@connectisra.co.il);
Danit Shemesh (danit.sh@spidimail.co.il)

Dear Tzippi and Danit,

Here's a question: are men and women allowed to discuss the Torah with each other? Can they wonder together whether the venerable King David in bed with a virgin might be construed as pedophilia? And Dina? And, oh! What exactly was Ruth doing at Boaz' feet... can this be raised in a *Shabbos Dvar Torah,* when the women who probably cooked the meal are present at the table?

Or is the Torah not 'pure' enough to be discussed in mixed company?

* * *

First, Danit, let's set the record straight: I didn't feel that I was "boring you" nor that I had "exhausted the subject." Someone asked me why I introduced Shakespeare into my book. I replied, and I stand by my answer, that *For the Love of God and Virgins* is about spin, about the unfair media rap Israel gets in the foreign press. Shakespeare was a master of spin; understanding his manipulation of facts facilitates understanding the process of delegitimization we are facing today.

I would love to answer your points one by one; I'm afraid I don't understand them. What readers of mine are over-sexed? And are you accusing me or Shakespeare when you wonder if he "can think about nothing else and so writes it all incognito?" Are you seriously claiming all Shakespeadre can think about is sex? Have you read him? And what did you mean by "incognito" – are you referring to the controversy over who wrote the body of his work... or do you mean 'innuendo?' You'll excuse me for not refuting your points in order; they're too confused for me.

Tzip, we will never convince each other of the validity of our views. But I'll summarize mine for the record:

Recently a New York Hassidic newspaper, *Der Zeitung*, expunged Hillary Clinton from the iconic White House photo of President Obama and his team watching the Pakistan raid on Bin Laden. Where she sits was a blank space; a female staffer was also excised. A couple of months earlier, in the Holy city of Jerusalem, a Brigade of the Boys in Black was incensed at the sound of mixed singing (i.e. women and men's voices mingling on a sound system in a kosher restaurant in the Old City.) The heroes in big black hats swooped in to the rescue, cut the electricity to stop the offensive filth, and dumped the contents of dirty diapers over the food of the blasphemers, thereby sanctifying the Almighty, blessed be His Name.

This is my point: no-one in your bucolic *yishuv*, I imagine, would sanction such repellent behavior. Possibly no-one in Tzippi's living room would even condone cutting Hil from her moment of glory. But! And there's a big, big 'but': this crazy, hysterical puritanicalism which we encountered in your pleasant living room is the first step on a very slippery slope. Listen to what Danit has to say: she was embarrassed because I discussed things that her community does not do in mixed company, sex is not a subject they take lightly, "we don't banter about it, or joke about it, or try to understand how the neighbor is doing it. We, a group of mature, educated individuals, uphold the value that sex is intimate and should be treated intimately."

I am sad for you, Danit, that you can't joke about sex. It's such a fun subject about which to joke. But that's not my problem. This is: I was talking about sexual slang in Elizabethan England, goddammit, not doing a salacious striptease or describing the finer details of whatever prurient minds could imagine. 'Trying to understand how the neighbor is doing it?' Is that what happens in your community after discussing sexuality in great literature?

Has your world gone mad?

I think it has; and I'll tell you why this worries me: it impacts on my world and makes it a bad, bad place. First it's baulking at learning, in mixed company, that "to die" was Elizabethan double-talk for having good sex, then it's eschewing sharing a sidewalk with one of the opposite sex, or a supermarket, or a bus. That's just a short hop away from separate concerts where women can't hear men sing (or vice versa), and separate plays, and separate lives. One tiny jump and we're burning bins and chucking nappies of excreta onto food contaminated by taped music that's treif.

I have one more point to make, before we move on, if we can. If I believed for even a second, for even a nanosecond, that this exaggerated purity led to less gender violence, more genuine love, better family values and deeper respect for women – okay. But does it? The ultra-Orthodox have gaily flapping laundry spread over their cramped balconies in *Mea She'arim*; it's harder to find facts and figures on spousal abuse. I'd guess that in societies that permit discussions on Shakespeare's double entendres, the figures of violence against women are no higher than in homes where all mention of sex is banished in mixed company. The opposite, I suspect, is true. Jerusalem taxi drivers report that a majority of clients visiting prostitutes are Haredi men; this anecdotal evidence does not constitute fact. Rabbi Elon, who sodomized his young *bochers*, probably denounced public discussions of sex. One bad rabbi does not a community tar; neither does excessive prudery result in 'good' behavior.

People are people are people. There are good people, and less good. There will be men who abuse women in any walk of life, across the board.

Talking about sex, and even laughing about it, does not change the statistics.

Can I convince you?
– I think not.
Can you convince me?
– Certainly not.
Where does this leave us?
– I'm not sure.
Is hysterical puritanicalism how we want to shed our light unto the nations, pelting them with poop if they miss our message? Is that what God would want?
– I can't believe it. Not for one tiny second.
God gave us His Torah, and He told us to read it. Did he tell us to read it in separate rooms from our sons and their friends?

I must have missed that part.

Pam.

From: Danit Shemesh (danit.sh@spidimail.co.il)
To: Pam Peled (pam-peled@bettaletter.com)
CC: Tzippi Sha-ked (tzippi@connectisra.co.il)

Dear Pam,

It seems to me we are speaking of two different topics. I was not referring to sex in literature or your book, or Shakespeare's interest in it. You're right, I'm not in any position to do so. My subject was talking about sex in Tzippi's living room in front of men and women who deem themselves observant Jews. This is akin to me coming into your living room full of your friends and neighbors and talking about the importance of dressing modestly even in the heat of summer, and not chatting up men except for one's husband. How would you feel about me talking about something that is of questionable relevance to your crowd?

Every speaker needs to know his audience in order to truly touch them. I felt you wanted to teach me what I should and shouldn't want to discuss. It was very interesting, but I would have preferred less talk about sex and more about spin. Our book is about why we each chose our way of life and how we feel about specific issues. It's not about changing anybody. It's not a forum for fury or debate. I don't even see a need to agree on anything. It's about being different, yet being fine with that.

By the way, Haredim can talk about sex all we want in the context of the Torah. Through the biggies, we learn about sex, and teach our children about it. However, there are guidelines to this learning, just like for most everything else. Sex is no different.

Yours,
Danit

Then Pam felt compelled to present her case to the masses in the 'Jerusalem Post.'

OPHELIA: BEIS YA'AKOV INNOCENT OR FOUL-MOUTHED WANTON?

By PAMELA PELED

THE SCENE: A multi-cultural food fair in Jerusalem's Old City.

THE CRIME: 'Mixed' background music piped from a kosher Jewish stall; i.e. women's voices mingling with men's over the airwaves.

THE PUNISHMENT: The Boys in Black Brigade swooped in to the rescue, cut the electricity to stop the offensive filth, and dumped the contents of dirty diapers over the food of the blasphemers, thereby sanctifying the Almighty, blessed be His Name.

THE PROBLEM: Nearly forty years ago, when I was a student at the Hebrew University, the English Department was housed in Givat Ram. I can't recall exact details of my studies; I think we congregated in the Lauder building near the lawns, and I remember floury pitot from the cafeteria, and coffee served in Styrofoam cups. But one thing jumps out of those wonderful introductory lectures to English literature: the day when two first-year students flounced out of Shakespeare I, grumbling vociferously that they hadn't come to Jerusalem to study pornography.

They were religious young women; one, at nineteen, already wore the head covering of a married matron, the other, the ubiquitous under-the-knee denim skirt favored by the modest

What had so offended their delicate sensibilities was Shakespeare's sonnet CXXIX – "The expense of spirit in a waste of shame."

"Spirit" was Elizabethan slang for the ejaculate, and our professor dissected the poem, explaining how it was an excoriation of sex. It's a graphic sonnet, number one hundred and twenty-nine, with its description of sexual congress as "perjur'd, murderous, bloody, full of blame, / Savage, extreme, rude, cruel, not to trust." The words are mimetic; the oohs and ahhs of the epithets imitating the sounds of love, and the plosive consonants adding to the fun. I was mesmerized by this first-time encounter with the power of words; the flouncers were appalled.

Over the years I have taught Sonnet CXXIX many times; and many a time and oft religious students have upped and outed from my class. Now I know that the kids from my class of '75 (one of whom went on to have nine children of her own), would never arm themselves with a dirty diaper and unfurl it over a table of (kosher) food. Nor would my nice newly-religious college student who reluctantly tore himself from the Shakespeare class once or twice, and then cracked and stayed to watch the balcony scene. He would never contemplate condoning such behavior; I am certain that he, along with all decent religious English Lit students would decry the mere notion that black-coated hooligans could dare to foul the sanctity of Jerusalem with smelly pampers.

But here's the rub: There is, in my opinion, a growing connection between stomping out of class when Shakespearian slang offends, and some pretty weird stuff. Let me explain.

A month or so ago, in the crazy run-up to Pesach, I was taken to task not for the stringency of my kashrut, but over some scurrilous Shakespeare. My interlocutor was from a small village that includes inhabitants known as Hardalim, a new word for me. Nearly 40 years in the country and, until recently, the only Hardal I knew was yellow, usually from Dijon, and came in a bottle. This appellation has nothing to do with mustard – it's an amalgamation of Haredi and *dati leumi* (national religious)... go figure. It seems as if the old secular-religious divide in Israel is passé; new distinctions embrace finer nuances. Hardalim go to the army and work; their men are not obliged to have beards, but their women cover their hair and never wear jeans. Oh, and mentioning sex in mixed company, even Romeo and Juliet's balcony blast, is beyond the pale.

In a bucolic neighborhood in the center of the country, someone from a Hardal community had read my novel, *For the Love of God and Virgins*. The book is about the unfair media spin against Israel in the foreign press, and William Shakespeare is the king of spin. I discuss, in the book, how facts are not facts until they are broadcast on prime time TV: audiences abroad hear about a massacre in Jenin and they believe it; the late-night retraction is missed or ignored. Goldstone says IDF soldiers kill civilians intentionally and that becomes gospel; by the time he changes his mind, the minds of millions are set in stone.

My reader proclaimed that she had loved my book. But there was just one little thing. She hoped I wouldn't be offended, but, please, could I consider writing an "expunged" version, one that she could show to her 19-year-old daughter, her mother and her 92-year-old gran. If I could just knock out a "cleaner" novel for a more religious readership, I would sell more copies.

I was flummoxed.

"What would you like me to expunge?" I inquired.

"The explicit sex," she explained.

Thus my confusion: There is no explicit sex in my book.

"It's the Shakespeare," she clarified.

"You explain that for Elizabethans the word 'nothing' meant anything to do with sex. You point out that Ophelia was flirting with Hamlet; when she says 'nothing' to him their banter goes from bad to worse."

This was offensive to my reader and she didn't accept my interpretation. Her Ophelia was a chaste, innocent Beis Ya'akov seminary girl, and the cruder variant had ruined the play for her. She did not want to inflict this travesty on her family. And, what's more, as I was informed later, the sexual proclivities of Shakespeare's characters was not a suitable subject for debate in mixed company; I had erred in introducing the topic where men were present.

Only hours later, as I was falling asleep, did my answer come to me. Are Beis Ya'akov daughters, and their moms/grannies allowed to read the

Bible? The venerable King David in bed with a virgin? Noah uncovered and incest between Amnon and Tamar? Judah and his daughter-in-law? King Solomon and his concubines? And so on and so forth. What exactly, for example, was Ruth doing at Boaz's feet... is that not a little too explicit for comfort? Should there be an 'expunged version' put out, one suitable for women and kids? And one more little thing: Can the Torah be discussed in mixed company, or is it insufficiently pure? "Forget it," advised a woman with whom I work, and whose kids have become Hardal. "There are extremists in every walk of life; she's not representative."

"Forget it," suggested a good friend, who is FFB (*Frum* from birth.) "It's not that we are prudes. It's just that discussing sexual slang in the early modern period, in mixed company, is the first step on a slippery slope."

Apparently, according to the more religious mindset, talk of 'impure' topics across the gender line leads to the sorry state in the secular world where sex is meaningless and some mothers worry if their daughters are still virgins at the age of twelve. Yes! That's why, according to her, in some secular bubbles, "many, if not most" non-religious Israeli pre-teens have sexual partners (to their mothers' relief.) Talking about immodest subjects in the living room is a direct cause.

To me there is something very wrong here, and very frightening. Now I'm not suggesting for a moment that hysterical puritanicalism leads to chucking dirty diapers at people who offend you. Nor do I think that all the devout are dogmatic; on the contrary, I value much that religion has to offer to the individual, and to the State.

But somehow a climate of craziness is creeping into the mainstream, in the guise of purity – no mention of sex in mixed company first, and then no mixing at all.

In certain segments of the population I believe that nursery schools are now gender separated, adding to the brouhaha over separate seating on buses, separate sidewalks, separate supermarkets in case, God forbid, a male arm brushes up against a female hip as he reaches for the milk.

Where is this written? And how are we letting it happen? If I could believe, for even a nanosecond, that this exaggerated purity led to less gender violence, more genuine love, better family values and deeper respect for women – okay. But does it? The ultra-Orthodox often have gaily flapping laundry spread over their cramped balconies in Mea She'arim; it's harder to find facts and figures on spousal abuse. I would hazard a guess that in societies that permit discussions on double entendres in Shakespeare the figures of violence against women are no higher than in homes where all mention of sex is banished when husbands and wives are present.

Can this obsession over purity possibly lead to a climate in the country where a group of Haredi heavies, incensed at the sound of women singing along with men on the sound-system of a kosher restaurant in Jerusalem's Old City, cut the cables to the amplifier and poured excreta over the plates? "They're a tiny minority," is always the cry, "a tiny, crazy minority who don't represent anyone except themselves."

I'm not so sure.

I think that in some genteel living rooms all over the country sparks are being lit for a most unusual way of life...where life can't be lived in mixed company.

Recently, a New York Hassidic newspaper, *Der Zeitung*, expunged US Secretary of State Hillary Clinton from the iconic White House photo of President Barack Obama and his team watching the Pakistan raid on Osama Bin Laden's compound in progress. Where she sits was a blank space; a female staffer was also excised. Down the line this bizarreness must surely translate, must mutate into something more sinister: bombing transgressors of gender separation with loaded nappies, for example, or setting their garbage cans on fire.

It seems to me that there's a burgeoning extremism spreading into more and more communities – separate concerts for men and women, separate youth movements, separate lives. Can this be what God had in mind when he charged us to be a light unto the nations? The question remains: Can women be present at a *dvar Torah*, say, at a Shabbat cholent lunch, when the question of Dina's unsuitable dalliance is raised? Can Song of Songs be studied when both mom and dad are around? Or is talking about this part of the Torah together the first step on a slippery slope to perdition? It's an interesting thought.

From: Tzippi Sha-ked (tzippi@connectisra.co.il)
To: Pam Peled (pam-peled@bettaletter.com)
CC: Danit Shemesh (danit.sh@spidimail.co.il)

Dear Pam,

It was a great idea – our project. It's in utter free fall now. Instead of trying to dialogue you're using it to vent your hatred of the Haredim – over and over again.

You know *full* well that of the 45 people there that evening only a couple of women (Rebbetzins) had a problem hearing about "spirits" and "nothing" in mixed company, (which was disrespectful of you in any event.) It's an utter distortion to state that that was the general consensus. I gave you "all the feedback" that came to my attention. You ignored the positive and harped on the negative.

You asked the audience for suggestions to "spread" the word and one was to clean up the sexual references in order to "sell" it to religious Jews and Christians. You know your audience was trying to be helpful. There was certainly no "climate of hysteria."

That, however, is not the point. The point is that we have embarked on a project that would be better served if:

1. We are open to dialogue and changing our minds.
2. We remain respectful of the other.
3. We can hold a critical mirror to our own communities.

The main issue is sensitivity. Pam, like you might decide that it's inappropriate to wear a tennis outfit for *Shul* – when you speak in front of a religious crowd it might be best to refrain from references to orgasms and ejaculations, Shakespearean or otherwise. *Especially* when you were kindly asked to do so. I believe one should always err on the side of sensitivity.

You call not discussing sex in a mixed crowd "hysterical purtanicalism." Do all roads that suggest discretion lead to the Talibanization of society? What a quantum leap of imagination. That's not even a slippery slope – that's free-fall into non sequiturs. Moreover, the Torah isn't crude or crass. You're correct; it mentions sex but chooses to couch talk of this nature in a sensitive and modest way (i.e. Adam 'knew' his wife.)

You misquote me as imagining that discussing sexual slang in mixed company, is the first step on a slippery slope. "It leads to the sorry state in the secular world where mothers worry if their daughters are still virgins at the age of twelve. Yes! She knows for a fact that 'many, if not most' non-religious Israeli pre-teens have sexual partners, (to their mothers' relief.) Talking about immodest subjects in the living room is a direct cause."

I did not say that. I told you about my 12-year-old relative, an honor student in a secular school near Ra'anana, who seems quite credible. She states that most of the girls in her class have boyfriends with whom they are physically involved. Her mother found nothing wrong with this and thought it was a valuable experience for her daughter. This may be only one mother's thinking; I don't attribute this mindset to the entire secular species. But I believe that at least one class of 12-year-olds in Israel is having a merry time. I also suspect such experiences are far more pervasive in the secular world than in religious enclaves, though I can't cite statistics.

You write: *"If I could believe, for even a nanosecond, that this exaggerated purity led to less gender violence, more genuine love, better family values and deeper respect for women – okay. But does it?"*

Well, Pam, at least one study reports:

> "According to the Central Bureau of Statistics data, despite their economic situation, it would appear that faith and observance give the religious and ultra-Orthodox (the Haredim) a happier life. 96% of ultra-Orthodox are pleased with their lives, as opposed to 87% among secular Jews. Among the religious too, the percentage of happiness is high: 91% of them said they were happy with their lives, as opposed to 86% of those who define themselves as traditional."

There's more: According to Catherine Rampell, from the *New York Times* (Jan. 2011), on average Jews have higher levels of well-being than their counterparts of every other major faith in America, according to new data from the Gallup-Healthways Well-Being Index. The most religious members of the Chosen People score highest.

The reason for the commandments and the stories you quote in the bible is that there was a need to negate what was rampant and acceptable. Like it or not, the bible mirrors the human condition and withstands the test of time. News flash: Not much has changed. Man still covets other men's wives, there are still false idols, and kids still dishonor parents.

The '*chup*' is the methodology and sensitivity in teaching these lessons. There's a time and a place for everything, as Danit suggested. The fact that some idiots sporting *kippot* twist/distort/ignore the central message of the bible while purporting to be *holy*, doesn't negate the message itself.

While I've attempted to address some of your points, I fear you have ignored or distorted many of mine. Ultimately, Pam, it requires desire and discipline to develop new attitudes, not to merely lash out and attack the other. I invite you to an evening of wine and cheese with a few ladies to discuss responses to our memorable evening.

What sayeth you?

– Tzippi

(We decide to continue with our project, in spite of the fact that the women of the *yishuv* did not want to meet with Pam. They felt she had an agenda, was tremendously unfair to them, and had presented a completely skewered, distorted view of the proceedings in the"Jerusalem Post.")

Chapter Six

A Jewish Mother in Israel

Tzippi writes:

> *"God could not be everywhere, and therefore he made mothers."*
>
> – Jewish Proverb

I was pregnant with my fifth child and had just returned with my family from a summer holiday in Israel. We were back in Los Angeles in scorching weather.

"Let's jump in the pool," I suggested to my eleven-year-old daughter, Ciona.

We swam and my heavy belly and aching back felt a relief that I hadn't experienced in months. The water was heavenly, the landscape blissful... it was good to be back.

"Isn't this wonderful?" I asked.

"It's all right," Ciona responded, flatly.

I knew that Ciona was unhappy about leaving Israel.

"Why can't you be happy to be back in L.A.?" I asked. "It doesn't get better than this!" I was floating on my back and irritated. Surely she was diving prematurely into moody teen years?

"It's O.K., mommy, but it's not Israel," she said.

I could sense the exasperation creeping into my voice.

"What is it that makes you so unhappy about leaving Israel?"

Her answer was an epiphany.

"Mommy, Israel is where you can ask big questions and actually get answers."

It was as if a cold splash of water hit me in the face; it wasn't chlorine that stung my eyes. Ciona was the wake-up call to our Aliyah. If she could search for meaning at such a tender age and tie it in with our love for Israel, we figured we were doing something right. In her words, "Didn't *Ha-Shem* give us a land so we could live in it?!"

A year later, we watched our children acclimate in our new home, Israel. They had learned the language and embraced the freedoms of *yishuv* life. Orie forgot words in English. Tehila and Chanan played in Hebrew; their English often sounded infected with a trace of something foreign. Only Ciona and Matan clung to their native tongue.

That first year I was so anxious about the move. Why was I not reveling in their new Israeliness? Because, I reasoned, it came with a familiar price. I thought back to my cultural disconnect from my own Israeli mother, and hers from her Persian one. While not an emotional estrangement, there was a tangible divide. Would it be the same between my children and me?

My kids were slipping into their Israeliness and I was driven to keep them culturally/linguistically tied to mother-America and to us. I was a mother on a mission, securing a shared alphabet with her offspring, panicking when I believed we hadn't taught them enough, hadn't worked hard enough to sustain the Anglo umbilical chord. Would my children morph into individuals seemingly unrelated to us? Generation gaps are part of life. Still, hadn't we encouraged this by inviting another language into our relationship?

Why do children scream they just "don't get you?" When do shared mental and linguistic coordinates dissolve and disappear?

Seven years later, I realize those worries were just small change. My hopes and fears for my kids took on a new direction.

These days I worry more about existential than linguistic threats. Nuclear-rabid Ahmadinejad is breathing down our necks. We have water shortages, Islamic terrorism, kidnappings of Israeli soldiers, internal dissension, corrupt politicians, an inundation of African refugees, and an international community that wants to sell us down a river without any flotation devices... there are definitely days when I know we were certifiable for moving to this complicated habitat.

Since becoming a mother, my perception of 'place' in the universe has changed. We moved to Israel for the sake of the children, to impart cultural and religious continuity. Life in Israel is largely lived on roller skates; it's fast! History unfolds at a dizzying pace and we sense that we are on borrowed time 'but for the grace of G-d.'

When I consider my role as a Jewish mother and the legacies I wish to leave our children, I think of the lessons imparted by the late Schijveschuurder parents.

In August 2001, six members of the Schijveschuurder family were blown up in an Islamic terrorist bombing at Sbarro Pizzeria in Jerusalem. Eight-year-old Hanna Schijveschuurder awoke from this nightmare and gave the following radio interview:

> "...and nothing will be just for nothing because the Lord knows what he is doing, and he wants to tell us that we need to behave a little better and soon the Messiah will come."

I think often of Hanna's parents. In this world we can't control what happens to us but we can lead by example. The Schijveschuurders had no inkling they would depart this world so inconceivably – while chewing pizza with their family. To have left their daughter resolved to forge ahead in the face of adversity, to have instilled a sense of hope, was the greatest legacy they could give her – in her parentless world.

As parents, we care for our children in myriad ways: providing education, a financial future, and even a good name. Yet, if they were to find themselves alone and rudderless, the greatest gift we can bestow is the sense that there's a higher system in this world. They are ultimately never alone; their maker watches over them.

Our move to Israel was, in no small part, due to existential deliberations. And while it can be tough here in terms of physical well-being, living as Jews in the Diaspora is tougher on our spiritual longevity. Pam, Danit – we do share ambitions as mothers. We each strive to nurture, preserve, and propel into the future – *our future* – our dear children. We give thanks when we see them blossom, and we hold our breath as they reach scary milestones. We pray for their health and happiness. True, Pam, we differ. You say Danit's way of life poses an existential threat to your own. Danit, you say entirely the same thing about Pam's. But, while we all stem from that same basic building block of humanity, *Hashem* has found a novel use for us all. Uniquely, Jews have so often managed to live in an amoral world, while upholding the best of Jewish ideals. We have learned to live with many dissonant chords, while still making a difference in this universe. Our real secret has always been our ability to support each other. That is so missing today. So, as we sip lattes I ask: how can we teach our children mutual respect when we ourselves don't have it?

I remember spending a Shabbat in a Jerusalem hospital. The emergency room was so crowded that patients were sleeping in the corridors. It was a religious hospital, so most of the nurses working on Saturday were Muslims. I watched one bring a stack of chocolates to the nursing station and the party started. When a Jewish nurse appeared, a Muslim examined the ingredients and handed over a bar: "It's the right kind of Kosher for you," she said, in Hebrew, and smiled. The Jewish nurse dived into the chocolate with a smile.

This easy camaraderie between the orthodox Jewish nurse and the Muslim staff was amazing. All it took was consideration, a smile, and some chocolate.

We Jews have a gift with words; we aren't called "The People of The Book" for nothing. Yet Jews are so quick on the verbal draw, unleashing a power through words that is very difficult to retract. Who are we to judge perceived weakness or strength in our fellow Jews? We need to teach our children: "There walks a Jew, who is a part of our nation." We have enough external threats. If we empower internal extremists who seek to damage us all, we become less governable and far less intact as Jews.

We *should* show patience, humility and a regard to the challenges the other may face, even when we don't agree with everything they say.

And always offer chocolate.

Pam writes:

A JEWISH MOTHER

I am a huge Paul McCartney fan; at twelve I plastered my cupboards with every Beatles picture I could find. Years later Martin knocked on my door on a blind date, and I opened it to find a McCartney look-alike, wanting to take me to dinner. I fell in love with him before his "hello." Life was lovely when I was twenty-seven: my parents had come on *Aliya*, my architect dad found a fabulous job, the country was almost at peace, and I was engaged to the perfect man. "I'm so happy," said my mom, clutching her head in her hands, "*kein anhora, kein anhora, kein anhora.*"

The plea to avert the evil eye fell on deaf ears; my darling dad was diagnosed with lung cancer before the wedding invitations were received; we had to call and cancel on our friends. Martin and I got married in a hailstorm in my parents' penthouse; our family braved snow to celebrate with us through our tears. My dad had only months to live; more than wanting to be a mother I wanted to make him a grandfather. It was not to be. By the time my problematic prolactine levels had been sorted out my father was dead; my first-born came into the world soon after to give her granny something to live for, and to enable her mommy to smile again. Becoming a Jewish mother was complex for me.

But from the moment my baby snuggled into my arms I embraced her, and motherhood, with arms and heart and breasts and brain. I fed each child till their first birthday: as I was pregnant three times in three and a half years that meant bathing while feeding, and wiping bums while feeding, and cooking while feeding. I fed while I taught; a scarf demurely over my dairy as my young student tried to concentrate on the difference between "I walk" and "I am walking." I fed at the Shabbat table while dishing up the soup, I fed in my sleep. And then five years of carrying babies and having babies and putting babies to sleep were over, and Martin and I suddenly woke to find that our three stunning young women had all slept through the night, and were babies no more.

It is not an original thought that you learn to be a mother from your own mother. I learnt from the best. It wasn't hard for me to give up late morning lie-ins, and tennis, and my figure; my mom taught me that small sacrifices were pleasurable when it comes to kids. Early on I instated the dinner-time rule: from infancy my girls sat down with us to eat and we discussed our day, and the state of the world, and moral dilemmas. My mom would join us, and we'd eat, and chat, and laugh, and fight, and then they'd go to bed.

Like Tzippi, despite my desire to live in Israel and have Israeli off-spring, I wanted them to have the best of both their worlds: fluent

English, love of Monty Python, an appreciation of cricket and the Beatles. I read them Enid Blyton books, and sang "Twinkle, twinkle;" we took them to Cape Town and London and New York.

Being a Jewish mother, incredibly, is sometimes more of a challenge in Israel than abroad. We are a "seculardox" family who keep kosher(ish) and keep traditions, but we find God on the beach on Shabbat. Yet we were totally unprepared one Friday evening when my then thirteen-year-old youngest daughter came to us with a special request. "My Scouts friends are coming before our *peulah,*" she explained. "I want to do *kabbalat Shabbat,* but I don't want them to think we're religious. Can we do the candles and *kiddush* early?"

Martin and I were truly horrified. We gathered the family and discussed how Jews in Spain lit candles in the basement, lest their religion be discovered and they be put to death. We questioned why Joanna would hide our traditions, and that her daddy blessed her before the meal; what was the point of an Israel at all if this was the feeling in its borders? My daughter was convinced; we waited for her friends, blessed them too, and broke sanctified bread together with them. One girl declared her family had Shabbat rituals too; the other said she'd request it. But the secular/religious divide had never yawned so widely at me before. I wanted to be on the religious 'side.'

And yet, when I read all-too frequent stories like the one that hit the news in Haifa last week, I wonder whether mothers who inculcate Jewish pots and pans values, are helping or hindering their kids. The rabbi in charge of *kashrut* in Haifa has been charged of having a good time in all kinds of indecent ways, instead of checking *shchita* and *shmura.* The poor sods who paid for his *mashgi'aching* skills were subsidizing his fun life-style; they paid more for their chicken so he could cluck around in someone else's coop. I know, I know, I know that the rules belong to God and not corrupt religious leaders, and I know that assorted rules and norms keep us a community. But in Israel religion and state lie together in an uneasy bed; things are cockeyed. Even being a Jewish mother.

I can relate to many of Tzippi's points, but one of her central tenets eludes me. Her talk of "the lessons the Schijveschuurder parents provided" simply confuses me. I can see, oh how well I can see, that believing in God can help individuals face their pain. Sometimes, when my beloved husband is writhing in the agony of cancer, and terror and suffering suffocate me, I wish that I could believe that God had a plan. It would be a comfort indeed to think that illness, traffic accidents, drowning, and murder were all part of the 'greater good' mapped out by the Almighty, Blessed be His Name. But would I want to believe in such a cruel, barbaric God? Why would He place a bomb on a bus full of Haredi children on a school outing; was their parents' *Shabbos* observance not strict enough? Did a trickle of milk manage to squeak into their *cholent*? Or is God a Shakespearean trickster, as Edward claims in *King Lear:* "As flies to wanton boys so are we to the Gods; / They kill us for their sport." Why would I want to worship such a God?

Let's not even get started; that subject horrifies me. I've seen parents on religious *yishuvim* thanking God for saving their children from terrorist attacks, while parents who were not so lucky say resignedly through their tears, that God is great and God decides. It's a win-win situation for God: someone is saved and He's responsible, someone dies way, way, way too young and it's part of the Plan. In my heart of hearts I can't believe that anyone really believes this in their heart of hearts, but who knows what fear and brainwashing and Jewish parents who knock this superstition into their children can achieve. I don't want my children to believe in an irrational, vengeful, cruel and incomprehensible God. I want them to believe that the Jewish people has a long and checkered history, and that they, by virtue of their genes and lineage, are a part of it. I want them to have fun with the traditions, and find their rhythms within the festivals and the holy days. I hope they have peaceful Sabbaths, and preserve a modicum of *kashrut*, in the spirit of an ancient tradition. But I hope and pray that I never indoctrinate them to believe that God is in any, any, any way at all involved in the fact that their daddy's beautiful body is now ravaged with his battle against cancer. That would be a sin.

I don't want my babies to use God as a cop-out; to justify their way of thinking. We brought up our girls to be critical thinkers, analyzing all sides of issues, realizing that life is complex and nuanced. The "God is on my side" syndrome enables multitudes to make decisions without compunction – Haredi Jewish mothers, for example, teach their children not to go to the army as "God is opposed." He needs them studying in safe environs. Hilltop youth invoke God when they burn cars of army officers; rampaging vandals invoke God as they burn garbage bins. I don't want to be that kind of a Jewish mother; I don't believe in that kind of a Jewish God.

Chicken soup, now that's something that we can all agree on, no? Do you guys blenderize the carrots, or leave them whole? *Kneidles* the whole year through, or just on *Pesach*? Let's debate the merits of a good bowl of broth – there we might come to some conclusions. On a consensus about life and how to live it we might have to work a little longer.

Danit writes:

AN IMA

Speaking of music, Pam, my favorite song as a teen was "*Dust in the Wind.*" Remember? Looking back, I'm horrified at how in sync I was to the song's message. Life, and the people in it, had no real meaning for me. I was no different from the next particle of dust, not special in any way. I had to outshine, outsmart, and outstand in the crowd. If I didn't, I'd be blown away because *nothing lasts forever but the earth and sky*.

Sure there was a game-plan to 'one-up' others: go to university, get a degree, then another, and another; become a professional and make a mark in this G-d forsaken world, get married to another huge professional particle of dust, make lots of money, stay gorgeous, have two kids, stay gorgeous lest your husband looks at cuter dust. After all, there are plenty of *fish in the sea*. Oh, I almost forgot: never to blink because then everything *slips away* and, in the end, *all we do crumbles to the ground though we refuse to see*. If you don't blink, you can try to hold off the crumbling away.

I ran from one project to the next like a packman, gobbling up my first college degree, then marriage, then my second degree. I was staying gorgeous. I was manager and owner of my own health club. I was doing it! I was a 'success,' working on schedule according to *The Plan*. You go, girl!

And then, I blinked. The miracle of motherhood stopped me in my tracks with a screech. In this state of quiet the Blink was almost too much to bear. The white noise of daily bustle was overridden by a deeper knowledge that I had been given a gift. I looked deep into her eyes and, dare I say, saw the higher Source who sent her into my arms. She was not a particle of dust in the wind. Her light shone through and the world awaited her arrival. I know babies are born everyday. What made my first-born any different? Nothing! My baby was a miracle like all babies, and it was my job to make sure she knew that.

So I made some changes.

I was blown away by our connection. Beyond my new motherly instinct to protect my baby from car fumes, hard rock, and overly-perfumed laundry soap, I felt an urge to know *Truth* for her sake, if not for my own. I owed my child a reality of hope and truth, of stability and borders, where she felt safe enough to know her real name and her purpose in this world.

Being a mother is so much more than checking for MSG in soup, teaching what is politically correct, and allowing a child to make her own way in life. It's being part of a historical chain which began with *Hava*, the mother of all life, and will last to the end of time. It's a divine gift that must never be taken for granted. It is my job to lay the stepping stones for my daughter to become her own being, with her own purpose.

I remember my great-aunts and grandmother sitting around the coffee table recounting horror stories about family members who suffered in life. Life huffed and puffed and blew their houses down leaving a pile of dust, a story of ashes, to be told to later generations. Through the old ladies' eyes I realized life is the luck of the draw.

My job is to weave my past and my children's futures with that insight; life is a collection of miracles, not a threatening dust storm. The thread with which we weave is Torah. The Nation of Israel has survived the centuries by being plugged into its Source: its safety net, framework, code of behaviors, and in-depth philosophy which takes into account the grandest of pictures. The Nation of Israel is on firm terrain once it is tethered to the Torah of Israel in the Land of Israel.

Yes, the rules are rigid and unquestioned, to truly anchor the nation of Israel. Did you think true serenity comes with no price? I offer my children an inflexible formula, because I truly believe there is meaning to their lives. Each of them has a story to be told, and that story will not be told to the fullest without a Torah framework.

Once the code of behavior is in place, the person can stop flailing about and grab life with both hands. We need to be part of something greater than us. I brought them into the Haredi community where the rules of the game are very clear. Once you have the manual down pat, you can be creative and individualistic; you can shine your own personal light. What is important to me as a mother is to invite my children to play their unique role as members of the Jewish nation.

When my twelve-year-old girl asked me about having children of her own one day, I told her that G-d is in charge. When it's time, she'll be ready. She is already preparing physically with her menstrual cycle, and spiritually with her prayer, learning the rules before she begins playing the game. Childhood is groundwork for marriage. You learn to compromise. You learn the importance of covering your body, embodying what you truly are: a princess. You learn to say 'thank you' to The King before every morsel of food enters your mouth and 'thank you' for 'good plumbing' after you exit the bathroom. I almost forgot that you need to learn that G-d gave you a special gift (apart from your body) called Shabbat. On the Sabbath you stop chasing white rabbits and just sit and enjoy the quietude and wholesomeness.

I told my daughter that my job as her mother is to teach her the rules, and help her commit herself to them. The One who will give her the baby provided rules that have been passed down throughout the generations.

Before my ten-year-old goes out to play, she must recite her morning prayers. Before my fifteen-year-old goes to her friend, she must hang up laundry. Before my twenty-one-year-old daughter self-actualizes, she must marry. It is via marriage that she will learn what it is to truly give and bond. To remember who you are you first remember where you came from, and that your foundation is Torah.

My fifteen-year-old's version of a night on the town is a walk around the neighborhood with a friend. My seventeen-year-old girl knows the rules about talking to boys. My twenty-year-old son knows that the woman destined to share his future will come with the heavy involvement of his parents and Rabbis, the people who most care for him. None of my children has internet, and movies are limited. Their social life is varied and rich; they have opportunities to be creative and inventive. Their priorities are clear.

The biggest problem for me is that both the secular and nationalist worlds appear to my children as ever-so sexy, so free. I, as a mother, know that true liberation comes from strong roots and clear do's and don't, but looks do deceive, especially the young. On the surface, shorts and sleeveless T-shirts look comfy and weather-appropriate in this land of sun. Having access to the world's latest technology is dazzling. Seeing the world as your oyster can give one a high. 'Living it up' is a high, from which one, by definition, always comes down. Life is about responsibility, stability, and prioritizing. I have nothing against the marvels of technology, as a means to an end. But an 'end,' in and of itself, implies something missing. That is what I must instill within my children. As the Talmud says: "The entire world was created just for me" (Talmud – Sanhedrin 38a) which is exactly what makes me responsible for it.

People prefer the path of least resistance, where comfort is revered and boundaries are considered *treif.* They embrace the philosophy of: 'I feel like it' or 'I just want to live it up.' This inviting path whispers in your ear sweet nothings about being progressive and liberated, but it leaves your children the task of reinventing righteousness and justice.

The core difference between us, Pam and Tzippi, is how we view boundaries. The Haredim revere boundaries as the formula to good living. Boundaries between parents and children enable the parent to do his job: parent. An awareness of what is and is not allowed in relation to food, activities or dress, enable one to design one's life according to thought, rather than base desires. We walk a fine line, questioning which behaviors are appropriate for a Jew. If *Torah* is our teacher and guide, we are reminded that there is a line not to be crossed, lest we become unrecognizable as Jews.

Pirkei Avot, a behavioral guide written by our sages, discusses a person's most important trait. Rabbi Eliezer says 'a good eye' or viewing people with loving-kindness. Rabbi Yehoshua says it's 'to be a good friend,' and Rabbi Shimon says 'to have foresight.' Rabbi Eliezer summed it up and declared the most important trait is a *lev tov*, a good heart. This includes all other virtues. Our Rabbis today have decided a good heart is cultivated in a nurturing environment void of influences that sully it: the violence, lies, and indecencies splattered across TV screens. So we keep them out of our living rooms.

In addition, our Rabbis have forbidden our children access to internet, cell phones, or gadgets which will prematurely expose them to the profane, and inhibit real human contact. Our children still play jump rope, five stones, and cops and robbers. We have also decided to distinguish ourselves in dress.

Once I took my children to *Gan Sacher* in Jerusalem. An ice cream man with a funny hat and a jingling trolley was calling out, "Sarale, Yaacov, Itzchak come get some ice cream! Where are you, Yehudit, Davidi and Tamari!?" The Pied Piper was reeling in the kids at the park. The children were astounded that he knew their names. We name our children based on our history, the foundation of our existence; we sing our heroes. Naming a daughter after a sexy actress hardly gives her appropriate tools to navigate this world. Making up a name because it's pleasant to the ears is misunderstanding what the child came to this world to do. It's a missed opportunity to give her a proper foundation.

When I kiss my kids goodnight, I pray to G-d they will know where they came from, to whom they are obligated, and where they are going. I pray they will have clarity of vision and the good *middot* to survive this world and to repay G-d for the good bestowed on them. If the ground is fertilized with an understanding of their importance in this world, as well as their obligation to it, not one of them will feel like dust in the wind. Rather they will feel cherished, protected and purposeful.

Rabbi Hakavia Ben Malalel said in the Gemara, 'you must know from whence you came, a putrid drop... and where you are going: to the dust... and to Whom you will be giving *din vecheshbon.*' In other words: yes, you are small in the scheme of things, but G-d expects the best of you, He believes in you. One only believes in one who is worthy of belief.

From: Pam Peled (pam-peled@bettaletter.com)
To: Danit Shemesh (danit.sh@spidimail.co.il)
Tzippi Sha-ked (tzippi@connectisra.co.il)

Hi Tzippi and Danit – I read your Chapter 5 with interest, Danit – the thing that struck me was you were so vocal about "Dust in the wind" and not wanting your daughter to feel like that: the phrase, of course, comes straight from Bereishit 3:19 "In the sweat of thy face shalt thou eat bread, till thou return unto the ground; for out of it wast thou taken: for dust thou art, and unto dust shalt thou return" so it seems that God Himself meant us to feel the futility/fragility of life... no?

Then you end with Rabbi Hakavia Ben Malalel himself predicting that we will end up as dust; maybe you didn't have to give up on Dylan?! It seems as if our Jewish balladeer got it all right, after all.

In the meantime, all existential and metaphysical questions aside, I wish you both a very happy, healthy and lovely end to the summer – good luck with the start of the school year, work, kids, family, homes and visitors!! And health, health, health to all.

With love,

Pam x

From: Danit Shemesh (danit.sh@spidimail.co.il)
To: Pam Peled (pam-peled@bettaletter.com)

Yes Pam, you're right about the fragility of life, in fact, Avraham Avinu said to G-d just before he argued for Sdom, "... and I am dust and cinder (or ashes.)" He meant he was in no position to approach G-d as a mere mortal who would go back to dust after death. Yet he did approach G-d with a request not to go through with the destruction of Sdom. It is true, Pam, that we must feel the fragility of life and of our own beings, but that is only vis-à-vis G-d Himself. For He is the Eternal and we are the finite. However, when it comes to this world or other mere humans, each of us must say, "and the entire world was created for me..."

There are two pockets with which we must walk this earth: 'I am dust and cinder' (to remember Who is in charge) and 'the entire world was created for me,' (to remember the centrality of our being here, to feel our enormous responsibility to the world.) Hopefully the two pockets somehow balance the person out so he approaches life from true homeostasis.

Chapter Seven

What we Know to be Treif: The Ladies Air out Communal Dirty Laundry

Pam writes:

WHAT'S WRONG WITH ME?

I know what you want me to say, Danit and Tzip, in this 'spill-your-guts entirely' chapter. What do I find wrong with my secular world? – Drugs, and sordid sex (stemming from the provocative, skimpy clothes of sluttish, secular kids), no family values, greed. And I agree with you. I'm not mad about random sex, gratuitous violence, drugs. The lack of family values, and community spirit, and kinship upsets me greatly. I'm all for Friday night dinners and 'so what did you do today' chats. But I'm not sure that the secular world is to blame for the breakdown of any of the above.

Yes, yes, yes. It bothers me that secular kids, many of them, feel the need to get drunk, often. I hate drunk – I hate the damage to the drinker and the damage it causes the drinker to wreak. Drugs frighten me; I feel saddened to think that kids (and adults too) need artificial stimulants to feel pleasure, or to feel relaxed. I don't advocate high school sex and certainly not with just anyone; violence makes me sick to the stomach. But are these ills of the secular world alone?

I'm not at all sure.

You have said – over and over again – that the way secular kids dress makes you happy that your world retreats under wigs and long skirts and the black robes favored by Christians from centuries past. I counter that physical and sexual abuse occurs in *Yeshivot* just as it does in the most secular space; and sexual frustration and deviance is as rampant in kosher homes as in those where milk and meat swim in perfect harmony in the same pots.

So, what is it that does disturb me about the secular world? The list is long:

- The sad women who are forced into slavery and prostitution
- The sad men who 'visit' those women
- Child abuse
- Wife abuse
- Poverty and deprivation
- Lack of intellectual and physical stimulation – a dropping off of the aspiration towards excellence
- Excessive competition on all fronts – pecuniary, physical, spiritual
- Alienation

I look at this litany of woes and readily admit: secular society suffers from them. But not exclusively. Yes, a disproportionate percentage of secular kids get drunk on a Friday night, swallowing vodka to fill the aching emptiness that comes from a hollow existence. Awful and tragic. And yes, some secular adolescents wear "screw me" shirts that barely cover their breasts. But here's the thing: according to Jerusalem lore more Haredi men service prostitutes than any other sector. We were all in Tzippi's kitchen when her butcher appeared bearing meat from Bnei Brak and told us (remember Danit? Remember Tzip?) that in that hyper-prudish, ultra-prim enclave of "sexual purity" his Haredi customers admit to being so starved of normal congress with the other sex that they imagine doing it with trees as they walk down their skimpy-t-shirt-free zones.

Friday night violence at discos, random stabbings and drunken brawls – all these I abhor and regret. But how many of these louts appear in court sporting huge kippot on their heads, mumbling *tehillim*? Don't rabbis ever abuse their young *bochers*? Come on! Some cases even come reluctantly to light in the secular press. The worst child-abuse ever in Israel, where babies were force-fed excreta and endured the unendurable took place in hallowed homes of Beit Shemesh, where an ear-locked rabbi and his modestly dressed supplicants beat the stuffing out of their children in very kosher kitchens.

People are people are people – with identical livers, and hormones, and synapses – no matter what their religious beliefs. People are people are people; there is good and bad wherever you look.

Let's take modesty. The secular world is not big on modesty; it's a problem. The constant striving after money, massive homes, designer cars and clothes and sunglasses: it's awful and it's sick. I'm 'richer than you so I'm better than you' is a horrible credo, and the secular world is much to blame. But here's the rub: do other worlds not hanker after better homes and bigger cars too? I presume a family of 14 in Bnei Brak cannot aspire to a Herzlia Pituach estate; but don't the parents ache for another room, a nicer couch, a more stylish *sheitel*? If you tell me hand-on-heart that the more religious you are the less acquisitive you become, really and truly, I'll concede that your world is luckier. I just can't quite believe it; I see rich religious folk with villas that vie with any in Pituach. Haredi women in New York wear gorgeous clothes, don't they? And diamonds? Bigger and better than those of their friends?

Let's take competitiveness – a not entirely negative trait. Competitiveness can build excellence, but in excess it can hurt. My society is excessively competitive; but is it exclusively so? True, secular pupils might lose more sleep over getting into Med. school or Law, or a crack unit in the IDF; but competition is an ingrained human trait. I know little of yeshiva life, but don't kids there strive to be "the best," the brightest, the one the Rabbi loves the most?

Secular women might well obsess more over cellulite and weight; spending more hours at the gym and plastic surgeon than their pious sisters; to me it seems that those women often vie to be the most unattractive in the group. That's a form of competition, no? The most shapeless skirt, the loosest tummy, the tennis shoes that least match the shirt? But there is a more insidious side to religious competitions: the competitive purity, or competitive *kashrut*. How long before *Pesach* do *you* start cleaning? Do you do the bathroom tiles? You wait only three hours between meat and a milky cup of tea... wow, we wait six – it's our *minhag*. There's killing competition in every society – trust me.

Poverty and deprivation? Surely not the prerogative of the secular world.

I grant that in the secular world there is more alienation. "No man is an island, intire of it selfe," said Donne, in 1624. "And therefore never seek to know for whom the bell tolls, it tolls for thee." (Meditation XVII.) Everyone wants to belong. Everyone wants a club, a football team, a group, a community. A uniform. So there are Scouts, and Manchester United, and choirs and Tai Chi. There are army units and school reunions and reunions of ex-pats from cities and countries and states. But the ultra-religious have this community built in, uniform included. Hari-krishna shave their heads and wear long, flowing gowns; the Orange people are clad in the color of their creed. The ultra-pious Jews sport long, flowing beards and the garb of oversized penguins. They look identical, merge into a crowd, are indistinguishable in a group. They pray in groups three times a day, and they sway and chant and feel like one. And that is what people crave – look at me, and look at me with you! I belong, we belong, I belong!

The ultra-pious don't have to work at creating family rituals: they have Friday nights and Holidays and the food and prayers on tap. Other Jews can dip into the ritual-box: we say *Tefilat Haderech* before each trip, and Martin blesses the kids each week, on the phone, if he's abroad. Our *kashrut* would place a miserable last in any competition, but we have our milk pots and meat pans and plates and cutlery for both. We "change" for *Pesach*; although not everything; our toaster and bread bin go into the shed. Ritual is lacking in the secular world – that sense of 'self coming from a greater-than-self'…and it's important. Alienation leads to the ache of emptiness; the aching emptiness leads to drugs and crime. That's definitely wrong with my world; we have to work harder to fill the aching void. *Daven* three times a day in the company of the like-minded and like-dressed, and the void will temporarily vanish.

How to incorporate ritual and belonging without the dogma and the dress is the challenge that faces the secular world today. It's a tough call.

Danit writes:

INTROSPECTION:

Introspection, what a wonderful concept. If we only focused inward more, hatred would be a thing of the past. I can see it now, can you? A new, improved world (after the coming of Mashiach), able to embrace difference, unafraid of the other. A world able to sustain the seventy faces of the Torah, in which all the colors of the Jewish rainbow coexist. No finger pointing, no ridiculing or demonizing; a world of brotherly love. Imagine... (Yes, Mr. Lennon, I am.) We're in the future – in a board room – watching a bunch of head honchos discussing bridging gaps. Suddenly one bangs his fist on the table yelling, 'this smacks of Israel 2012! I will not stand for such backward behavior, ostracizing and blaming!'

Back to reality. Like you say, Pam, I know better than either of you ladies what's wrong with my community because I 'live' it. Most of your views on our lifestyle are oversimplified and grossly misunderstood. That doesn't mean the Haredi community is perfect. I'm certainly not blind to its imperfections, I live here fully aware of them.

The community business is, by definition, flawed. Any community – from the bohemian in Tel Aviv to the ultra ultra whatevers in Mea Shearim – swallow up individuals for the good of the whole. The community can only survive if individuals feed it pieces of themselves. It is a symbiotic relationship which, for the most part, works. Nudists ask members to peel off layers of social standings, (hey, Pam, did you catch the one about 1000 Israelis disrobing, exposing, shedding all inhibitions for the sake of art at the Dead Sea this weekend?!), the Kibbutz asks to relinquish private ownership, the University asks for excellence and competition, and bohemians ask you to go with the flow. There's a price to pay for belonging to a community, a price we accept. If you feel forced to comply with another's dictates, that's when the trouble begins.

I am tested on a daily basis, and I'm still here. I walk down the main street of my community, waving and smiling at people I know, and I feel I am home. Yes, there are challenges: just the other day, I needed to go to the *makolet* and hoped I wouldn't run into anyone I knew, so I could go in my sandals. Then I realized that was ridiculous. I put on socks because that's the norm here; women wear socks, even on hot days.

Yes, I know, Pamela, you'll see this as backwards and anti-feminist and, truth be told, I hate socks. But it's not just socks, I don't much like black or blue attire either. There's definitely something to what you say, Pam, that the competition is to be more modest rather than sexier, and the side-effects are shapeless skirts and oversized penguin suits – a definite eyesore for the more visually inclined. But, on the other hand, my yeshiva-student son in Bnei Brack can't walk down a certain street where girls dress provocatively and he feels like he's in a scene out of "Clockwork Orange." What's more offensive? Tents and socks, or too much skin? I suppose it's a matter of perspective.

Still, life lived in a community can feel just a bit overwhelming. When a community takes life so seriously and sternly, good moods are less obvious – although not non-existent. Yet, when I walk through the streets of Tel Aviv each week when I lecture to university students on Judaism, I see faces in that city that are just as stern. There aren't enough smiles . . . anywhere.

And yes, I see exhausted women with a parade of ducklings toddling behind, running all over in mad disarray. She (the Haredi woman) – in dire stress – is trekking up a steep hill, or negotiating traffic with her motley crew. I also see dirty children on the streets playing with nothing but a beat-up ball. The children seem perfectly happy; it's the mothers I wonder about. Life should be great fun, as well as serious work. Purposefulness and righteous behavior should not negate having good times.

How did you know, Pam? The week before Pesach is the maddest, baddest time of the year for the Haredi woman. You walk down the street and hear yelling from the houses: "Shoshi, I told you to go outside with that cookie!" or "I can't believe you didn't check if the toothpaste is kosher for Pesach!" I have learned never to go to the *makolet* just before Pesach as I will be accosted by a woman in socks asking how my cleaning is going, even before she remembers to ask how I am. If women answered truthfully how they felt before Pesach, they would say "harried, frazzled, uptight, and overwhelmed." Instead they answer "*Baruch Hashem*," as if that answers anything. The week before Pesach, I send my only-too-willing-to-get-out-of-the-house husband to the *makolet*.

Truth be told, I was always more suited to a foot-loose and fancy-free environment, something Hippie-like with no rules, no ownership of the individual, where no-one is forced to wear socks. In a Hippie community anything goes; everything is celebrated.

In the Haredi community we live by a basic tenet: we are *not* allowed to do anything, unless we *are* allowed to do it. Are we allowed to eat that, listen to that, watch that, be with that person? Are we allowed to read that or say this? Are we allowed to represent this or speak up for that? Yes, we live in a state of what you, Pamela, would term fear; I call it 'mindfulness.' This community enforces care and behavior modification. In my weaker moments, I daydream about bohemians who don't hover over me, where everything is permitted, except for what is not. In my community the feeling of pressure and 'right and wrong' is like Jiminy Cricket breathing down my neck, waving his little finger at me and telling me I'm bad. Then, I get slapped back to reality, realizing that Hippies no longer exist. How did they raise their children with no constitution of behaviors? Is it possible in this day and age to loosen the grip, or do we need to be extra careful so that both children and adults will not fall into complacency?

Tradition takes precedence over many politically correct ideologies. The Haredi community is Topol up on a horse and buggy yelling at the top of his lungs "TRADITION!!" – only not in such a lovable manner. Tradition allows the Sephardics to eat legumes and rice on *Pesach* whereas the Ashkenazis are forbidden from doing so. This protocol heralds back to the fields in Poland, where the mixing of wheat with legumes and rice was a common practice. The Arab countries maintained separate fields and could dish up *Pesach* legumes with a clear conscience. The joke about town is that the Sephardics need to recite *selichot* for over a month because they eat *chametz* on *Pesach* and that the Ashkenazis need to mourn over the destruction of the Temple for three weeks (as opposed to nine days) because they enjoy suffering and are infused with extra doses of Jewish guilt.

There is more painful introspection that I will share with you, in light of the Tal Law. It has to do with the boys in yeshiva who don't go to the army. I believe with all my heart that this country, as well as the international Jewish community, needs serious boys who learn and make a 'home' for G-d down here. There are certainly boys who are not serious and who go to yeshiva to avoid conscription. Most of the yeshiva boys, however, are diligent learners and I'm proud of them and their commitment to connecting the lower to the upper world, making a home for G-d down here for the rest of us who are either protecting the front line or having more Jewish babies.

I've described the side-effects from which my community suffers as a direct result of being good 'soldiers' and taking the task at hand seriously. We are here on a mission: devoting ourselves to G-d's decrees down here in the trenches. We need to stay focused. It is because we are at war (be it with the Arabs; amongst ourselves; within our respective homes or even with ourselves) that we need the manual – the Torah. This manual brings the Chief of Staff into our own home.

We can never forget that life is not a dress rehearsal; nor are we in a simulation cockpit. While we may have many chances to perfect ourselves, it would be better to get it right the first time around. The job of the community is to maintain boundaries. The job of the individual is to adhere to these guidelines and to truly live, enjoy, and be his own person. The question that I ask every day is: can I truly be my best self with loose Hippy-like boundaries, or do I need a firm hold so that I can feel safe?

From: Tzippi Sha-ked (tzippi@connectisra.co.il)
To: Pam Peled (pam-peled@bettaletter.com)
CC: Danit Shemesh (danit.sh@spidimail.co.il)

I received your chapter. Thank you. My feeling is that you kindly wrote introspectives for everyone else.

From: Danit Shemesh (danit.sh@spidimail.co.il)
To: Pam Peled (pam-peled@bettaletter.com)
CC: Tzippi Sha-ked (tzippi@connectisra.co.il)

Hi Pamela,

I must admit, I was very uncomfortable writing this last chapter on introspection. It's no easy task, hey? Maybe it's especially difficult for me because I feel I'm representing something that's up against the wall, facing the firing line. I want to be honest but I don't want to mislead or face your 'seeeee, I told you!...'

I wrote it itching and sweating and am not sure how it will be received. I was honest and that comes with a price. I was wondering, however, Pam, if you truly looked deep inside and came to terms with 'what's wrong with your community?' I'm curious because your list is dire and a recipe for self-destruction; you cite lack of meaning for teenagers, internal emptiness, overly zealous competition, prostitution or mistreatment of women, and so on. How can you have time or energy left over to deal with other communities' problems? I'm not being funny, it's an honest question.

Danit

From: Pam Peled (pam-peled@bettaletter.com)
To: Danit Shemesh (danit.sh@spidimail.co.il)
CC: Tzippi Sha-ked (tzippi@connectisra.co.il)

Hi Danit – I'll need to rework my chapter as I obviously didn't make myself clear. My point was that the list of "dire" ills in my society, and the "recipe for self-destruction" is *not* exclusive to the secular world – I believe that people are people are people – and sexual dysfunction, competitiveness, mistreatment of women exists *across the board* – regardless of one's amount of 'religiosity.' Sure, not all Haredim are sexual perverts – just because some are – and not all secular kids are vacuous either, just because some are. Religion makes *zero* difference to purity of the soul and goodness – there are good and bad 'religious' people, and good and bad secular.

I had lunch on Thurs with a religious friend of mine – her 2 sons both grew up very, very *machmir* – yeshivot, hesder – the whole toot. Today one is gay (and anti-religious), and the 2nd, a 33-year-old handsome hunk, is totally anti-religious and professes that all he wants from life is to have sex with as many women as he can. Both her boys, she told me (and she is still religious), completely blame their 'pure' yeshiva upbringing for making them sex-crazy. I wonder whether your son, Danit, is aware how bizarre it is that he can't look at a girl's elbow – what would happen to him? Would he not be able to control his repressed lust and think – (gasp!) – of having a few minutes of wonderful, pleasurable sex? Oy yoy yoy. Or would he feel the need to rape her? Just like Ayaan Hirsi Ali describes the Muslim men – and the Muslim repression – and your description of always being aware of a power above watching is *exactly* what the Muslim girls are told – there's an angel on their shoulder, watching for a stray bit of shown skin. It's just tragic, in my opinion... those poor kids!! Whew. How do people who know differently embrace this madness?

Laila tov and love,

Pam

From: Tzippi Sha-ked (tzippi@connectisra.co.il)
To: Pam Peled (pam-peled@bettaletter.com)
CC: Danit Shemesh (danit.sh@spidimail.co.il)

Dear Pam,

Many thoughts about this last chapter: While we both agree that what is happening with the Haredim is frightening, we approach the problem from different vantage points. You feel anger and dislike, I rather feel heart-broken that Haredim can't see the *ikkar* from the *tefel*. The Haredim are arming for battle but losing the war regarding uniting *Klal Yisrael*. Tragic. I am torn because they seem so blinded. I want to repair the damage, not decimate the perpetrators.

I do hope, Pam, that at the end of the day we aim to really hear the other and not merely air our separatist views... I'd like our work together to reflect more depth than merely three broads breaking bread, inhaling java and dodging bullets.

– Tzip

Tzippi writes:

"Knowing yourself is the beginning of all wisdom"

– Aristotle.

Whose side am I on? Must I decide? My secular cousins accuse me of being an apologist for the Haredi camp. My Haredi friends echo them regarding my views on secular Jews.

Frankly, I don't belong to any particular camp. I'm not even a genuine camper in the Modern Orthodox or Hardal movements. If anything, I'm a balanced critic of both.

I fear for the future of the secular Jewish narrative, untethered to the Torah. (I'll settle for Torah ideals if not halachic directives.) I'm appalled at an identity with little or no connection to Jewish precepts. Some secular Israelis view their link to their homeland as just an accident of birth. I don't see a future for an Israel populated by Israelis ignorant of, and indifferent to, Judaism. Secular vehemence against Haredim is at an all-time high. The sacred cows of tolerance and multiculturalism almost never extend to Haredim. Yes, Pam, secular culture *is* overly steeped in fashion, drugs, risqué movies, theatre and vapid television – the Western idea of pleasure *is* to flee the pain and loneliness of this world (yet you don't believe religious Jews are happier!) Activity is often misinterpreted for achievement, "fun" for meaning, and love is offered oh so freely. You acknowledge the problem, but you might not be aware of the repercussions.

I find it terribly sad to read of baby boomers aging into a state of depression. But why wouldn't they? After all, they live in a society that glorifies youth and vitality. Pam, there is far less of this *angst* amongst religious Jews, who enjoy greater inner contentment. While many secular view 'happiness' as a goal and a 'right,' for religious Jews it's a consequence of living by Torah ideals which provide 'ultimate' meaning.

But I'm a fair critic. I also decry certain issues of the Haredim. I agree with much – but not all – of what Pam says: Don't drag us back to the dark ages, you Men of Moses in black. Your movement is doing so, Danit, when it shuns the secular curriculum, imposes its views with verbal or physical threats, and resorts to emotional blackmail. Your community will never accrue bonus points by looking down on the Jewish authenticity of others, blocking roads on Sabbath, or manipulating political blocks in government. Let's not even talk about the rantings in Beit Shemesh.

But this chapter is not about accusing other sectors; it's time to turn for introspection of my own community.

While you, Pam, are sure most people don't voluntarily embrace Orthodox Judaism without some psychological disorder or emotional affliction (like running away from a turbulent past,) I beg to differ. As renowned British anthropologist Mary Douglas suggests, the yearning for laws and boundaries (call it rigidity if you want, Pam) is universal.* Humans gravitate towards hard lines, structure, and clear concepts. We're even apparently wired for it. In Israel, as secular Israelis deviate from tradition, Haredim become more stringent. Pam contends this is also true of the Modern and Hardal communities. I concede that this might be true in terms of Jewish ritual. Although I don't want to believe that Haredi philosophy will triumph, I fear she may be right.

I believe that both the Hardal and Modern communities do not have clear delineations for where they fit into the halachic spectrum. While I identify with the Modern/Hardal view that secular education is compatible with Holy learning, I don't think it always succeeds. Modern Orthodox teens are often so enamored of secular pop culture that they adopt secular dress codes and conduct. Many Modern Orthodox teens make out in public, dress suggestively, floating on booze and spewing trash from their mouths. Laws of Modesty are often dismissed. Sabbath rules are bent to enable texting friends, and drugs circulate in that world with fairly easy access. I agree with Pam, that some of the problems in secular society plague ours too.

What's happening? I suspect the chief cause is the breakdown of the family structure, in every community. With mom and dad often out of the house, parenting gets lost in the daily shuffle. The Haredim celebrate a culture where the wife is the breadwinner, so half a dozen or more children find themselves in a house alone. In our own community, teens sense a disparity between what they learn in school and how their parents live. Forget internecine fights across the Jewish denominational divide – our community is battling over its own identity.

Modern Orthodox Jews and Hardal subscribe to a philosophy of halacha of convenience. If the halachic injunction fits their world view, they embrace it. If not, it's relegated to the status of an inconvenient ideal. At worse, it's rejected outright. Often teens resist fitting their philosophical choices into Judaism's prescriptions. But, if you pick and

* Douglas, Mary. Purity and Danger: an analysis of the concepts of pollution and taboo. London: Ark Paperbacks, 1988.

choose your halacha, you get a 'pick and choose' culture. Sometimes it's good to be modest, sometimes not. Sometimes it's good to abstain from premarital sex, sometimes it's inconvenient.

Young people in the Modern Orthodox movement seem conflicted. It's great to be part of the larger world but, they say, it's difficult/unnecessary to filter out the offensive. The lines become blurred. Recently 1,000 people gathered at the Dead Sea for a mass photo event in the nude. I wondered whether Modern Orthodox Jews opposed the shoot as vehemently as the Haredim?

The Modern Orthodox rule book includes an admiration for infrastructure, but blurs hard lines and halachic concepts. We, in the Modern Orthodox/Hardal world, should realize that our religious foothold is slipping, together with our *hashkafic* grip on our children. We're in danger of losing them to the Haredim on a ritualistic level or to the secular on a cultural one. At the end of the day, as the non-Orthodox deviate further from Judaism, the Modern Orthodox may become more Haredi, preferring that to a secular stoop for our kids. This worries me.

I am prepared to do something about it. Both paths (the Haredi and the secular) are a nightmare for me. Religious identity is at the heart of Jewish survival and I think the Modern Orthodox have that down. I thank G-d for certain Haredim who keep scholarship alive. I cringe at others who believe they are the sole gatekeepers of our faith, and who create a society void of secular scholarship and productivity. On the flip side, secular Jews don't worry about G-d. *He* simply does not exist. That, too, is worrisome. How did we get to the point, Ladies, when we view fellow Jews as the enemy, as a threat to our own survival? That is just as scary to me.

Pam, you want evidence that being religious is worth the trouble? That it actually leads to a better way of life? Well, research proves that religion seems to make people happier. That when humans believe in constant accountability to one's maker, they tend to be more just, more generous, and happier.

The Gallup-Healthways Well-Being Index, calibrates the happiness-scale of Americans. The Index's statistical composite for the happiest person was: "A tall, Asian-American, observant Jew who's at least 65 and married, has children, lives in Hawaii, runs his own business and has an annual household income of more than $120,000."

At least we struck gold with the observant Jewish aspect. But an index alone isn't reason enough to embrace religious Judaism. Perhaps this is: living in a religious community, while not ridding us of problems, mitigates the sense of confusion, and lack of direction.

In addition, both in Israel and the States secular Jews are demographically threatened. They are at risk of assimilating into obscurity. While that may be good news to some calloused Haredim, it's terrible news for the Jewish people. The intermarriage rate among secular, Reform and Conservative Jews is proportionately greater than for the Orthodox (72%, 53%, 37%, and 3%). So here's the bottom line. Whether you like it or not, if you want Jewish grandchildren in the Diaspora (and soon perhaps in Israel,) your only bet, is to enroll them in Orthodox Jewish Day Schools. Research confirms that stronger Jewish education and adherence to Jewish law lead to lower intermarriage and assimilation rates.

From: Pam Peled (pam-peled@bettaletter.com)
To: Danit Shemesh (danit.sh@spidimail.co.il)
CC: Tzippi Sha-ked (tzippi@connectisra.co.il)

Hi Ladies –

I started the year with tennis *al haboker* – what could be better – and over my granola breakfast read the "Jerusalem Post"... and now it's official. See Page 2 – 'Taking on the Taboo.' Atzum, the organization fighting prostitution and sex slavery in Israel, estimates that 10,000 Israelis visit prostitutes each month – 25–35% of clients are Haredi – 25–35% Arab, 8–10% foreign workers and the rest regular Israelis. Haredim are up to five times more likely to pay for sex than the secular men.

So where is the covering of hair, and wearing socks (shame, Danit – what a waste of effort!) to the *makolet*, and taking a different path (like your son) so as not to encounter an elbow... where is that leading you guys? And the answer is: straight into the arms of prostitutes.

Let's get this book out there!!!!
Love,
Pam x

From: Danit Shemesh (danit.sh@spidimail.co.il)
To: Pam Peled (pam-peled@bettaletter.com)
CC: Tzippi Sha-ked (tzippi@connectisra.co.il)

Hi Pamela – I understand your perspective, but I think that although our community goes to a lot of trouble to stay covered, there are still renegades. What prevails, prevails. However, it's not *because* of modesty.

Maybe secular society doesn't need to pay for sex. After all, post-feminism women have no problem going out to find "Mr. Right *now*." This, of course, renders prostitutes obsolete for the first time in history if I'm not mistaken. Yes, we are more closed off, but as you say, people are people are people and they will get what they need. Our way of life forces the periphery out, it does not mainstream it. The reason we cover up is that G-d commands it, not to curtail any behavior that can't be curtailed, as you correctly pointed out. The difference between our communities is that your peripherals are less obvious – society expands to contain them – while my community refuses them entrance; when they infiltrate they stick out like a sore thumb.

The truth is, it is kind of fun to talk like this. I really look forward to your letters. You have become dear to me and I appreciate your thoughts.

With good wishes,
Danit

From: Tzippi Sha-ked (tzippi@connectisra.co.il)
To: Pam Peled (pam-peled@bettaletter.com)
CC: Danit Shemesh (danit.sh@spidimail.co.il)

Pam, you state: "How to incorporate ritual and belonging without the dogma and the dress is the challenge that faces the secular world today. It's a tough call."

It's not a tough call. It's a mindful decision. It's the decision to embrace the middle ground of halachic Judaism, which is the only possibility of Jewish survival.

From: Pam Peled (pam-peled@bettaletter.com)
To: Tzippi Sha-ked (tzippi@connectisra.co.il)
CC: Danit Shemesh (danit.sh@spidimail.co.il)

I've done chapter 7, ladies... but I'm a bit scared to send it... are you up for it? Mmmm... we'll need a spiked latte after this chapter, and perhaps some boxing gloves... Pam xx

Chapter Eight

Paralysis? Army / Work / Politics

Pam writes:

SUSTAINABILITY

A few days ago, a police patrol was called in to Mea She'arim to defuse a suspicious looking object that could have been a bomb. God's work, one would think, risking your own life to protect others. Those young policemen were probably newly married, with babies at home; and here they were in darkest *doss* land, taking apart a parcel which could blow them to kingdom come, in order to save the lives of the neighbourhood Haredim. One would imagine, surely, that residents would welcome them with flowers and dates, or at least with smiles. But this is Haredi country; the officers were welcomed with rocks thrown at their heads.

Why? Police are not welcome in Mea She'arim. Neither are tax collectors, nor judges. Doctors who advocate autopsies are stoned too, or the Almighty is invoked to blot out their names. Law and order are not valued in this part of Jerusalem, unless it's the Divine Law of the (hairy) cowboys who live there.

In this chapter we look at sustainability: the status quo vis-à-vis the army, work, and politics. And here is my thesis: the situation in our Holy Land is unsustainable, untenable, and rotten to the core; it's the boys in black, and their servile womenfolk, who are largely to blame. If our implacable enemies were clever they would lie low for a generation or two, waiting till we were swamped with Haredim. Our army would be a shambles, our workforce decimated, our economy subsisting on handouts from wealthy Jews abroad. Fatah or Hamas or

Jihad or whoever is around in 2045 could just waltz in and overrun us; no soldiers to stop them, and mothers too busy nursing baby number twelve to notice. Let's tackle the issues one by one.

THE ARMY: Until perhaps a year ago I would have said the single biggest existential threat to the modern state of Israel is the Haredim. This population frowns upon joining the army, ostensibly on holy grounds. Studying in a yeshiva, we are told in all seriousness, throws a girdle of sanctity around our blessed land, keeping us safe from harm. How terrorists infiltrate these houses of prayer despite the protective ring of faith, indiscriminately massacring rabbis and *bochers* in their path, is not discussed. Alternatively these tragedies are accepted as "God's will," or "strange and mysterious are the ways of the Lord." It's a win-win situation for God, always.

Haredim don't do the army. Yes, today there is the Haredi Brigade, mostly for drop-outs from the National Religious Camp, and for a few renegade *Haredis* who have lost their way. A few bone-fide Zealots do doff their big black hats for an army beret, and slip out of their hot black gowns for the sleeker khaki get-up. But they are few and far between, and they get flak from their community. Pamphlets call to ostracize them, zealots beat them up. New legislation aimed at "equal sharing of the burden" – army for all – is threatening to engulf the country in civil war; only yesterday (22/2/14) one Rabbi Shmuel Auerbach, a leader of a hard-line Haredi faction, declared that his boys "will fight until death, literally" not to enlist in the army, where they might need to fight until death, literally, against Israel's enemies.

I am typing this having just returned from a terrible place – the military cemetery in Kfar Saba – where the 21-year-old son of my good friend lies buried. He was killed on Yom Kippur eight years ago, during the closing minutes of *Ne'ilah.* He was shot by a random, never identified sniper, at a quiet spot on the Lebanese border during peacetime. It was three days before he was due to be demobbed; his mom had already baked his homecoming cakes. She spoke today, my wonderful friend, of the aching loss that only gets worse, and of things unspeakable and dire, and then his dad, for the eighth year in a row, said *kaddish* in the presence of family and friends. The military rabbi intoned the haunting

El Maleh Rachamim – God who is full of mercy – and I had an epiphany. There is no mercy in God, but I was suddenly filled with a newfound respect for Haredi moms. They *know* there is no mercy in God, and they do their damnedest to make sure He never wreaks his brand of mercy on their kids. So they *shtupp* them into places of worship where they can be safe and warm and fed, and where they don't have to put their lives on the line for their country. And they say it's God's will, and no-one can prove otherwise. How clever is that?

Haredi moms and pops have the perfect cop-out for keeping their kids far from danger: God wants them to *shockel* all day in a yeshiva instead.

Of course He does.

What mother in her right mind would send her boy to Gaza? I'd be tempted to put my kids in black suits myself, if it kept them safe. Especially if I could lay the blame on God.

And then, when their boys are 21, they get married to other ridiculously young kids, and make more kids who will never endanger themselves in defense of the country for which they pray three times a day. And we, the secular who go to the army, send our kids to the army, and do army reserves till our hair is turning gray, we pay for them to sit and study about sex and violence and biblical battles.

Haredi moms.

Simply spectacularly brilliant.

If I always believed Haredim were Israel's biggest existential problem, today I think the National Religious movement is muscling in on the threat. "Religious" officers recently flouted army orders and left a room where female soldiers were singing, raising major issues of whether God or the Chief of Staff commands the military operations in Israel. "Religious" hooligans are wreaking havoc country-wide burning mosques, desecrating cemeteries and uprooting olive trees (all in flagrant defiance of the laws of Judaism); the religious mainstream is moving towards the loony hysteria of their Haredi counterparts.

And it terrifies me.

WORK: Yesterday I drove down Raoul Wallenberg Avenue in the Ramat Hachayal area of Tel Aviv, on my way to interview a stunning young woman who is doing magical work for Israel's image abroad. The area is a high tech hub – impressive buildings, sleek cars, sleeker young things in high heels chatting to gorgeous young men in creamy shirts – and loads of trendy restaurants. It is Israel at its best; polite driving, smiling people, entrepreneurship, creativity, innovation. It's a thriving, pulsing center of life; it makes you proud to be Israeli.

And there, in the middle of this buzz: a disturbance. Four young Haredi youth, ear locks flapping in the wind, came whizzing along on some kind of Heath Robinson contraption – pulling a makeshift trolley laden with *schach,* palm fronds for the roof of the *succa.* They looked strangely incongruous in that industrious zone; disheveled black trousers and grubby white shirts, thick glasses and wild hairdos, but that wasn't what disturbed me. These boys can only dream of owning cars, and paying tax, and earning a salary. They don't own the tools. They can't speak even the rudiments of English (unless their parents happen to be American), they don't know math, they haven't heard of chemistry, or saturation points of liquids, or that $E = mc^2$. Their computers, should they have them (which is unlikely), are wired to block any content that could compel – no sex, obviously, but no secular philosophy either, or evolutionary science. These poor kids! It's not their fault they are so disadvantaged; their moms are to blame, and their impoverished dads, who spend their days out of the golden sun, studying, studying, studying until they drop (or possibly visiting prostitutes.)

Haredim don't work; not if they're male. Their wives bake cakes to augment the family income, or teach, or work in factories or (wo)man phone lines. Some even work in high tech today, while their husbands study, study, study. And yes, things are changing slowly, drip by drip. More of the pious are entering places of work, and discovering the satisfaction of paying for the bread that they bless, instead of blessing the charities that donate it. But as long as our corrupt system continues to pay men to stay out of the work force by giving them stipends to study, the vast majority do just that. Stay out of the work force.

So we pay for them – my husband and I – and our children, and our friends. We work our butts off to earn enough to pay for our kids to go to university to become productive members of society – doctors and lawyers and teachers and pharmacists and architects – and we pay for them to sit and discuss the sexual proclivities of David and Jonathan. Etc. More fools us, and how brilliant are they! How did they make this system work?!

But, brilliant as it may be, sustainable it is not. One fine day the Haredim will wake up to find the secular forever fled from this workerless land, and their stipends will dry up. So they will need to work – but they won't have the wherewithal. That's when Hamas, or Fatah, or whoever so desires, can just walk right in and sit right down...and God help us then.

POLITICS: Oh man, politics. If there's one sphere that Haredim are totally into, it's politics. Where there's money to be scrounged, there are pious doing the scrounging. They don't fight in the army, but they are there in the Knesset, voting on whether our boys should go to war or not (and getting paid off hugely to vote with the Government coalition.) They don't work much, but they vote on economic proposals, and get paid handsomely to vote the right way. They can stop planes flying on Shabbat, and they can stop shops operating on Shabbat, and they can legislate that their schools should receive mega-handouts even though they baulk at teaching the State core curriculum. They use their clout to determine where housing is built and for whom, at what price, and what ancient bones should be saved instead of living people (as in the Barzilai Hospital Emergency Room debacle.) Oh boy. When it comes to politics they come out of the *Yeshivot.*

Sustainable? Not very likely.

But who knows...maybe it's all part of God's greater plan...back to the Diaspora for us for another couple of millennia or so, and then...*Moshiach? Moshiach?? Moshiach??? Lai lai lailai lai-lai!!*

From: Danit Shemesh (danit.sh@spidimail.co.il)
To: Tzippi Sha-ked (tzippi@connectisra.co.il)
Pam Peled (pam-peled@bettaletter.com)

Hi, ladies, I am perplexed by what you call sustainability. We've been raising children for umpteen generations and are still here to tell stories of heroism and triumph. Our approach has proven itself over and over again. At the risk of oversimplifying our *ani maamin*, the Haredi way is this: know your worth as a human being, and live by what is expected of you to the nth degree. You've been given tools for a certain job in this world, now do it, and do it with gumption. You alone are responsible for carrying your own weight and that of your children. No crisis is an excuse to renege on this; deal with problems and go back to work, unlike those who begin new movements when they can't handle the rules of their community.

In short, I'm not sure you ladies should worry about sustainability of the Jewish people if the Haredim "win the war." There is no Israel without Judaism and there is no Judaism without the Haredim. I'm actually not the one who said that, Yair Lapid said the same in his talk to the Haredi campus in Kiryat Ono. He also said that Israel was established by mainstream European secular pioneers hoping to build a land based on the idea that G-d looked away, and so now we fend for ourselves.

Well, ladies, times have changed. Fringe groups came along like the Moroccans, the Ethiopians, and the Haredim who sucked the life out of the secular mainstream, mostly because they believed that G-d made this land possible and so they wanted to keep the ancient way of life. You, the secular, have enjoyed center stage for sixty years now. You have created an education system, a government system and compartmentalized religion. Are you succeeding?

Reading your (secular) newspapers, let's do a quick survey of your education system. '34% of secular children finish high school.' In the same global study Germany came in first with 81%. Then there are other problems. Doron Mairi and Edna Adito from *Yediot Achronot* reported that 'Children under the age of twelve begin to use drugs.' 'In Tel Aviv there is no school clean of drugs,' say Tamar Talebasi Chadad and Edna Adito of *Yediot Achronot*, '62% of teens use alcohol regularly,' claims Israel Moskovitch from *Yediot Achronot*. Other headlines include a youth who 'killed his brother while drunk and was sentenced to eight years in prison'; 'a thirteen-year-old boy shot himself dead with his father's rifle'; 'a man kills his son in front of his wife'; '25% of boys in the Shfela went to school with a weapon' and 'Americans admit there is a direct connection between a violent society and TV watching.'

I have only just begun. Before you secular whimper about having us to deal with, straighten out your own problems. We're still waiting to be convinced that you are going to keep this country on the map.

Still love and respect you, only can't agree with you.

Danit

From: Tzippi Sha-ked (tzippi@connectisra.co.il)
To: Pam Peled (pam-peled@bettaletter.com)
CC: Danit Shemesh (danit.sh@spidimail.co.il)

Dear Pam,

It's taking me some time to calm down after your last chapter. I gave your chapter to a Modern Orthodox friend of mine with some concerns and complaints vis-à-vis Haredim. I wanted to get her perspective. She wrote:

> "This chapter terrifies me. I'm scared sick that YOU don't recognize how much this writer is brimming over with vitriol and antisemitism. She is vicious. And I'm NOT talking about the issues she presents! Do yourself a favor and show this chapter to someone else you respect and ask them to describe the author's character. As for me, spare me her despicable brand of hate. I never want to see anything else she writes. I have to take a shower now to wash away her nasty stereotyping."

Oh Pam! You fail to see what others do so clearly. I know and so does Danit that you are a lovely person with clear concerns regarding the status quo. Is there no other way to express them? The manner in which we discourse is as much the message as the expressed goal.

Yours with much regard,

Tzippi

P.S. Have you heard: A secular Jewish woman accosts a man traveling on a subway, dressed in hassidic garb. "I think you people are disgusting," she says, squinting. "I'm Jewish, too, but I don't need to broadcast it to the world! You stick out, you bring shame upon our people."

"Madam," he replies, in a soft voice: "I'm Amish."

The woman gasps. "Oh, I'm so sorry! I think you people are wonderful, how you hold on to your traditional ways..."

From: Pam Peled (pam-peled@bettaletter.com)
To: Tzippi Sha-ked (tzippi@connectisra.co.il)
CC: Danit Shemesh (danit.sh@spidimail.co.il)

Whew – just walked in to find this stuff... gulp. I thought the purpose of the exercise was to write what we really felt...

Read Uri Regev in yesterday's paper – "Social justice, religious freedom and the tent protests" – your modern orthodox friend will be shattered to see that 87% of Israelis share my views... are nearly 90% of Israelis vitriolic anti-Semites????

But, you know what... maybe you guys are right – we stupid seculars should leave the country to you – have fun! – we'll live in peaceful Canada or India or the Bahamas or somewhere... with our bikini-clad, immoral daughters and our army-serving sons... maybe we should all intermarry and leave Judaism to the 'real' Jews in wigs and black coats. I'm needing to write a book about this all... and go viral on YouTube with it... whew whew whew.

Love you!

Pam x

From: Tzippi Sha-ked (tzippi@connectisra.co.il)
To: Pam Peled (pam-peled@bettaletter.com)
CC: Danit Shemesh (danit.sh@spidimail.co.il)

Pam, why run to the press? Who commissioned the study you quoted? Hiddush? If so, was anyone in Modiin Illit polled? How about Beitar? Tzefat? Jerusalem? Bnei Brak? Statistics are easily manufactured. With all due respect, Rabbi Uri Regev is hardly an impartial pollster. He certainly is a 'Rabbi,' but one who has declared a veritable Holy War against Haredim. Moreover, one of the founders of Hiddush is Shahar Ilan, a former editor of *Ha'aretz* who served as the in-house Haredi-basher.

As far as leaving Israel, Pam, if you feel a strong connection to the Jewish people, you don't abandon them, you strive to improve them.

To what end would you want to make this go viral on YouTube? To broadcast to the non-Jewish world that we can't make it work? To give them one more reason to disdain the Jews? I don't get your motive.

Yours,

Tzip

From: Pam Peled (pam-peled@bettaletter.com)
To: Danit Shemesh (danit.sh@spidimail.co.il)
CC: Tzippi Sha-ked (tzippi@connectisra.co.il)

P.S. Another thing: The Amish work – and work hard. No other group in America supports them financially. This might be a reason that they are more respected there.

America has a volunteer army. So there isn't resentment against the Amish for not joining, as no-one has to.

That's 2 very large differences.

Shabbat shalom and xxx

Pam.

From: Tzippi Sha-ked (tzippi@connectisra.co.il)
To: Pam Peled (pam-peled@bettaletter.com)
Danit Shemesh (danit.sh@spidimail.co.il)

A full 36 hours without internet!!!! AAARGH!!! . . . Almost didn't cope . . . so Bezeq's timing to upgrade the entire *yishuv* got us smack in the middle of our cyber wars. I have only now re-connected with the rest of the planet, so please forgive me for not reading any emails in the past 36 hours. Phones were another problem . . . if not for this deity thing I would have made *yerida* long ago . . .

So let me catch up, between appointments. Is everyone getting along now? Is there more excrement hitting the propeller blades? I guess I'll have to peek at the emails – shall I take a Valium first?

Boker Tov, dear ladies. Danit got started on the next chapter. What do you think, Pam, should we give it a shot?

Tzip

From: Pam Peled (pam-peled@bettaletter.com)
To: Tzippi Sha-ked (tzippi@connectisra.co.il)
Danit Shemesh (danit.sh@spidimail.co.il)

If Danit got started on it then I think I should too – let's see if I can come up with something original. Am now p.e.t.r.i.f.i.e.d of sounding anti-Semitic... watch this space for a whole new me ..

From: Tzippi Sha-ked (tzippi@connectisra.co.il)
To: Pam Peled (pam-peled@bettaletter.com)
CC: Danit Shemesh (danit.sh@spidimail.co.il)

...but we like the 'old' u....

Don't disappear on us. Where is punchy Pam?

From: Pam Peled (pam-peled@bettaletter.com)
To: Tzippi Sha-ked (tzippi@connectisra.co.il)
CC: Danit Shemesh (danit.sh@spidimail.co.il)

---

ha. Wait till you meet the new one... I'm going to be all sweetness and light and the soul of compromise... you'll be sure the mashiach has already landed, and whispered words of wisdom in my ear...

Pam xxxxxxx

Tzippi writes

> *"A fanatic is one who can't change his mind and won't change the subject."*
>
> – Winston Churchill

SUSTAINABILITY? I AM MY BROTHER'S KIPPAH....

I approach this chapter with emotional fatigue. Pam's talk of Haredim as a veritable plague upon the Jewish people leaves little room for discussion. Yes, it's true, for the most part, Haredim are under-represented in the army and the work force, but times are a-changing. One day Haredim will work, like their counterparts in New York, Jo'burg, and

London. The Tal Law will impact on greater numbers serving in the army (incidentally what about the growing number of secular Tel Avivians who opt out of the army?) When Haredim arrive at this necessary juncture, you should not object to any role they play in politics. We both know that there can be no Jewish democracy in Israel without a large Jewish majority; only the high Haredi birthrate can sustain this.

Pam, you correctly claim that extremism can't work, and the greatest good for this country must include a sustainable army and a productive workforce. I too am upset with some Haredi positions, but I posit that what is missing in our entire discourse is an honest discussion of intrinsic belief.

There are two types of Jewish inhabitants in this land. Those whose raison d'être is Torah, and those who redefine a Jew as something more in line with Western sensitivities and sensibilities. The fundamental divide among our people is this: the sole purpose of creation for religious Jews is to serve the Almighty through Torah and mitzvot. For the secular it is to extract and reluctantly retain the 'utilitarian' aspects of Torah, (and only those aspects which conform to Western sensibilities and personal preference,) without accepting the belief system which informs it. You write, Pam, that you respect Jewish values, but I suspect that you'll keep these values only as long as they don't fly in the face of your comfort zone. In other words, picking and choosing Jewish values without ascribing them to *Hashem's* directives.

So here is the question for non-Torah minded Jews: If Judaism is not inherently authentic, why preserve any of it? Why have candles on Friday night, and *Kiddush*? Why eat *matzot* on Pesach? Is it for nostalgia that you preserve form without belief? Isn't this futile and empty? So, Pam, while some deviant Haredim frequent prostitutes, it's also true that every year 50,000 non-deviant Israelis backpack to the Far East looking for (amongst other things) spiritual validation. That's something they're not getting at home.

In the end, it comes down to doing our due diligence. We, as a Jewish nation, must decode who we are and why we're here in one of the world's toughest neighborhoods. If our game plan is to be like every other nation – but better – why not assimilate and become simply a technological wonder and environmentally-friendly pit-stop?

Are we here merely to chase accolades? I read "Start Up Nation" about our technological and military prowess and Nobel laureates and yes, I'm proud. Proud, but not dazzled. What's missing from our 'kudos' narrative is that our real prowess has always been our tight-rope act; perpetually balancing our Torah-centered faith while negotiating hostile hosts who want to divest us of our heritage. We've always faced a Hamas of one sort or another, yet we never reneged on our Judaism. We remained members of the Tribe. Not members of the Western Tribe or the Western Ideal Tribe. That is not what Jews signed up for in the desert long ago.

It's mind-boggling, but these days we ourselves are doing the dirty work, *we* are ridding Jews of their Judaism. Move over Ahmedinijad, you have nothing over some of our internal hatemongers.

What's missing in our project is what's also absent in our national discussions. Where is the real introspection? Where are the thinking secular citizens? Where are the thinking religious ones? To the secular I ask: where is this going to lead? Is your game plan mere numerical survival and technological supremacy? Is the secular notion of advancement staging Shakespearean plays for mixed audiences in Tel Aviv? Do our audiences need trendy, no trendier, no trendiest clothes, and to go home to 2.2 secular children parked in front of HD TVs? Is this nation-building? Or is it national erosion?

To the thinking Haredim I say shame on your failure to live to the highest Jewish ideals. You're playing with fire – irresponsibly! Your communities should model kindness and mutual aid to all people, as well as responsibility and concern, and make this irresistible enough to melt the toughest *sabra* heart. Sadly, none of this is happening.

Meanwhile, on the ground, the divide grows and deepens. This is where introspection and honesty become brutal. If one's ideal is to assimilate into the family of nations (with a superior technological edge,) then the Haredim pose an obstacle. The next step invites stereotyping and its ally: hatred.

But let's be clear. Which sectors have a genuine interest in sustaining Jewish survival? Who has the real interests of the Jewish people at heart? Secular Zionism, Modern Orthodoxy, Haredi Judaism? What is making our nation Jewishly unsustainable? Haredim not serving in the army?

Modern Orthodoxy feeling uncomfortable serving next to singing female soldiers? Yes, Pam, that happens, but when it comes to putting one's life on the line for the state, the National Religious sector is far better represented than any other sector. Statistics show clearly that secular Judaism has failed miserably to enhance Jewish survival. That said, can we in good conscience continue to be ostriches and cheerlead the Haredi ideology that is anathema to Jewish survival?

So is the status quo sustainable?

I think not.

Danit writes:

THE ULTIMATE SUSTAINER

Here we are on the most dreaded topic, the fat thorn in your already sore paws. I can understand the thorn, it's annoying and distressing. On the face of things, it does appear downright antagonistic that the '*boys in black*' don't join the army or work, but still manage to fly their flag high in the political arena.

Ladies, you picked three topics: the army, the workforce, and politics. I imagine you picked them because you view them as vital elements to keep the State alive. However, it takes more than that to sustain us. The bigger question is: what does each community contribute to the overall sustainability of the Nation of Israel?

Now sustainability is an interesting concept – especially since it is in the eyes of the beholder. What is sustainability? Is it purely the maintenance of the army, workforce or politics? Does contributing to society count: setting up charity organizations for the sick, poor, and handicapped? Or establishing a health system fully equipped for emergency situations with a task force like *hatzala*? Perhaps sustainability is setting up educational networks to help Jewish families know more about Judaism, free classes on *shalom bayit*, counseling teenagers and couples, helping families deal with... well, life. What about manning hotlines for calls from suicidal teens or their parents? What is that called?

What is sustainability? Is it picking up a gun and protecting the borders, waving banners bemoaning the price of cottage cheese, or working on a new scientific discovery? Can it be something less celebrated but equally important? Is it possible, Pam, that you are so busy suffering from the '*boys in black*' because of the repulsive physical specter they present to you, that you don't see what is right in front of your nose?

What does a society need to sustain itself? I'm sure it's all of the above. We need brave souls, as well as good-hearted ones. We need the smart and ambitious, as well as the empathic who hold the dying lady's hand in hospital, or tell the sick little girl a story. Who's to say what sustains us more?

By the way, the Haredi contribution is undiscerning about what kind of Jew it serves. We give unconditional help to all Jews. The Torah commands us to save lives, to treat Jews with respect, to give of ourselves, to care for the downtrodden. Haredi community service does not come from a fickle spurt of inspiration. It's based on a set of eternal rules etched in stone. We are devoted to sustaining Israel whether all Israelis like it or not, because we're commanded to do so. This help is totally trustworthy.

But, let's not stray too far from what's bothering you ladies. The biggest stumbling block for my case is the unfortunate merging of Judaism with the army/politics. They are strange bedfellows.

On the one hand, Judaism is a spiritual value system which keeps us good and whole. On the other, Judaism is not just a family album you sometimes pull off the shelf to remember that you're a part of something bigger than yourself. It's a way of life. If you don't live and breathe Torah every minute, you are missing the point. Judaism is not a set of suggestions for when the going gets tough. It's not a little old grandmother with hot chicken soup and good advice. I imagine your wrath when that same grandmother yells on TV about the desecration of graves, or that streets need to be closed on Shabbat. How dare she? She has overstepped her boundaries!

She dares because in her eyes her grandchildren are crossing a busy street without demarcated sidewalks. This is a dangerous world; the Torah is our protector. Torah is the reason for being, not an accessory to life. Granny is guiding and protecting her family and she'll stop at nothing, she'll cross all red lines, to keep her family safe. She feels the dangers that threaten her grandchildren and she becomes an Amazon.

If government, the army, and the workforce are an intrinsic part of life here, then they aren't strange bedfellows with Judaism after all. They're an integral part of our infrastructure, and need to be addressed from a Jewish perspective. I don't claim that the Haredim are Judaism's only possible representatives, or even the only protective grandmother. But when no one else wants the role, someone needs to come up to bat. They are the ones reminding the Jews of their origins and right to exist.

I believe that if your community, Pam, embraced Judaism more, my community would release the pressure and do what we really want, which is to stay in our own secure environment and not become entangled in politics or the workforce. We would be the sweet compliant grandmother. However, not only does your community deny its Jewish focus, it does everything in its power to be like all other nations. Sometimes I feel your community is afraid to stand up and say, "I'm Jewish, and in your face!" The fact that we are a *Jewish* nation is not parenthetical. Are we Jew*ish,* as in sort-of-a-Jew, or do we stand for something different? Haredim believe that we are first and foremost Jews – that's what makes us a nation. The Torah is the pillar of fire guiding us.

The bare facts are as follows:

- Israel is in a state of constant war
- We are few in number
- We are busy building a whole new world
- We need more money
- We have a very bad name in the global community

In short, I have to agree with Tzippi: the situation is dire indeed.

All of us are cognizant of these irrefutable facts. They obligate us to act. We are all in the same boat, with waves around us ripping and roaring. The difference between us, Pam, lies in our approach. When your community sees 'hostile Arabs' on the horizon, it calls on you to build a strong army and raise the 'never again' flag up high. Your community sees the need for global competition and expects members to hit the books and discover something new. You need money, so you go to work. You believe in a democratic government so you set one up, with good checks and balances.

That's all fair and understandable.

The difference is the Haredi community sees reality both on that pragmatic level as well as on a metaphysical one. We don't believe that the amount of time spent working correlates with the amount of money in your bank.

We believe that even if every Israeli picked up a gun – the aged and young, the women and girls – we would not be safe against the Arabs, if we relied on this pragmatic solution alone. All it would take to wipe us off the face of the planet, for example, is for every Arab kid to take a kitchen knife and start a Jihad against Israel.

We don't believe any man-made constitution will make justice possible or truly give every citizen free speech or dignity. Man-made laws are as flawed as their designer. Look what happened to the poor souls who believed with all their might that they were sustaining Israel by settling in "occupied territory." They trusted that they were doing this for the land, for democracy and look how the man-made policy treated them in the end. They were kicked out of their own homes! How flawed is that? The government was supposed to protect the heroes of the day! The true sustainers of this land! They turned their backs on you and made the army, another sustainer, pick you up forcibly and throw you into buses. How did that work for you? Are you in comfortable homes now, a decade later? Did you manage to sustain us? We cannot make this stuff up as we go along, kowtowing to the Americans or whoever is in charge. We need a written contract and not one written by any man, who is flawed by definition. We need an external absolute perspective to add our checks and balances. Otherwise, we're at the whim of politicians or the powers that be.

If I lived the belief that 'what you see is what there is,' and if I didn't believe in a metaphysical level of reality, then I would also be very upset and uptight. Like you, Pam, I would feel that things are not moving in the right direction and that something needs to be done. I'm not sure I would take the track of hate and spite, but that's another issue.

The good news is that there *is* another level of reality: the supernatural. This is the surprise, the miraculous, the unanticipated. If we viewed Israel's existence without it, we would scratch our heads in bewilderment: how could this tiny 'lamb' create her own little space smack in the middle of a pack of ferocious wolves?

Yes, we have to have an army; that is the way of the world. Yes, we need to work, or how else do we eat? *Parnassa* is also the way of the world. And yes, governments need to exist, that too is the way of the world. However, the minute I depend on these institutions for survival, I am dead in the water. No man-made institution can possibly explain the huge idea of the Israelites finally returning home after so many years of wandering, from all the corners of the world with different languages, different customs, different mentalities. Can the government serve us all? No. But back in the desert we all agreed the Torah is the one thing that would serve as our constitution.

It would be disingenuous to read the map of Israel solely on the basis of physical frontiers. We probably all agree that it is nothing short of a miracle or freak of nature that we're actually here at all. From the War of Independence with its disproportionate numbers, the odds were against us. Our men suffered from malnutrition and exhaustion. Only a belief in the supernatural can explain why we won every single war, for there is nothing logical there. Of course, I'm not detracting from our soldiers' incredible courage and strict adherence to authority, which also helped. But mankind needs to know our limits. The army is crucial, yes. Does it alone save us from being pushed into the sea? Here's the rub, as Pamela says in her wonderful South African accent: I wholeheartedly believe, as my brethren do, that the army is another tool of nature which G-d utilizes. It is not an independent high and mighty entity that answers only to itself and does what it deems necessary to get the job done.

My husband was a pilot in the IDF. A few years ago he went to a reunion. He was the only 'penguin' in the hall, but that didn't stop him from attending. He was, after all, in the company of his war buddies. A young whipper-snapper sergeant stood up in front of these heroes of the past, and with a fancy stick and a chart presented a pyramid qualifying the levels of the armed forces. The lowest were the infantry; the highest, of course, were the pilots! They get all the glory. The tip of the pyramid was the Air Force. My husband raised his hand amidst the nodding heads, some balding, all successful in Israeli society, though not in their marriages; they were mostly divorced or never married.

"Yes?" said the young sergeant, curious as to what on earth my husband had to say.

"What's above the tip?" my husband asked.

"What?" replied the stupefied young sergeant. "What's above? . . . nothing! The air force is the pinnacle!"

The only one who understood was astronaut Ilan Ramon, may he rest in peace.

He got up and said, "I have been higher than any of you and I can tell you, once you get up to a certain level, there is only you and G-d."

They say there are no atheists in the trenches. I would imagine that is true. The question is when is a good time to *let go* of cynicism? Is it only when the axe is at your throat? Before a dangerous mission? Perhaps when a young man is drafted? Or would a good time to realize we are not alone in life's endeavors be *right now*? Why wait for danger before believing in God?

At the end of the day, Pam, the question is emotional, not cerebral. When you claim I put my son in *yeshiva* so that I can sleep at night, the implication is so very selfish and cruel that I can only wonder at the anger that is consuming you. All that energy wasted on anger! How do you South Africans put it? 'Shame . . .'

Once I welcomed a group of Kansas businessmen to our small neck of Israel, the Haredi community. The organizer allowed the bus driver to ask me a question. He said, "My three sons are in the army. If any of them get killed, how are you going to feel?" The question was obviously not a question at all, but an accusation, complete with pointed finger. I answered that I would feel terrible, just terrible, if anything happened to one of his sons. Every Yid is an entire world!

However, if we look at an object from different angles, it will appear different. What you seek, that shall you find. If you look for natural consequences, you will find them, and be blinded to what may lie beyond. You may feel a certain satisfaction in being right, and sanctimoniously point your finger at my sons, blaming them for your troubles. But you miss the big picture: you need to notice the metaphysical level.

The *bochers* (as you call them, Pam) are boys who implore G-d to keep the Nation of Israel alive and well, not unlike Avraham Avinu did in Sdom. If we go to war with the knowledge of Who is in charge of your sons' destiny, we need to keep the channels with Him open. Those channels are Torah. No shortcuts. Torah is the raison d'être of our existence, especially in the land of Israel. Therefore I countered the concerned bus driver's question with one of my own: How would he feel if no-one learned Torah while his sons were in the trenches?

Moshe Rabenu held up his hands during Israel's fight with Amalek. As long as his hands were up Israel won, as soon as his hands came down, Israelites began to die. In *Sefer Shemot* it is written 'and the hands of Moshe are *emuna* (faith)' – they represent not the physicality of the war, but reaching up to higher spheres, where *emuna* wins battles. Reach upwards and you shall prevail, by proving you know Who is in charge.

All I know is that this has worked for Israel: one third of our survival depends on the front lines, one third on the decision makers, and one third on the sages who keep the metaphysical channels open. Are we truly so 'enlightened' that we no longer believe in the metaphysical? Are we like all the other nations who believe in the power of the sword? Would you want to face military situations without supernatural help?

You and I are in the trenches, where there can be no atheists.

An avalanche of emails ensues:

From: Pam Peled (pam-peled@bettaletter.com)
To: Tzippi Sha-ked (tzippi@connectisra.co.il)
CC: Danit Shemesh (danit.sh@spidimail.co.il)

That driver who asked Danit about how she would feel if his soldier-son was hurt speaks for ALL of us with kids in the army – including the modern orthodox. I, for one, wouldn't care at all if no-one was sitting all day studying Torah – *but why can't they do both – like the modern orthodox do????* And, if they did both, our secular world would embrace Torah much, much more – with open arms – because it wouldn't be seen as a cop-out for pale-faced yeshiva *bochers* who are evading the army. That bus driver must have shaken his head in disbelief at Danit's question.

Surely, surely, somewhere deep in their hearts, Haredi mothers like Danit (and your friend, who sounds like a bitter, twisted and vicious woman... shame, I wonder what her story is) must at least acknowledge that their strategy to keep their sons safe is somewhat skewered... or don't they?

From: Tzippi Sha-ked (tzippi@connectisra.co.il)
To: Pam Peled (pam-peled@bettaletter.com)
CC: Danit Shemesh (danit.sh@spidimail.co.il

Yes, we are so different, yes, we disagree, yes, the problems seem insurmountable…but hatred? You don't realize that hatred is seeping out of your piece; that is what I want to draw your attention to. My 'friend' felt it too which is why she became so defensive. You might be surprised to hear that I have friends who are Haredi to the max, Breslever, Arab, Gay, Goth, secular Jew, German, Lebanese Christian, anti-Zionist Jewish; I don't particularly agree with many of their viewpoints. Yet, we are friends. We relate to one another's humanity. And, on a personal level, we like each other. Pam, we are in danger of treating the other as less than fully human and I find that *terrifying*! It's so easy to find the 'ugly' in the other. If there are problems, work, *work* at affecting change.

I would love to see Haredi women become emancipated, and engage in the civil discourse in this country but I'm not sure there'll ever be a meeting of minds across the religious divide. The best we can hope for is dialogue. The day will come when Haredim are involved in army/work/academic institutions and when that day comes we had better have something other than hatred on which to create a relationship. Don't you think?

From: Pam Peled (pam-peled@bettaletter.com)
To: Tzippi Sha-ked (tzippi@connectisra.co.il)
CC: Danit Shemesh (danit.sh@spidimail.co.il)

Dearie dearie me.

How are you, Tzippi?

– I think I'd like to reply to the woman who was so vicious about my views…could you let me have her email? Or I could invite her for coffee…with you…?

Have just reread the email from your friend; another very weird thing…your Modern Orthodox reader says: *I'm scared sick that* you *don't recognize how much this writer is brimming over with vitriol and antisemitism. She is a vicious writer. And I'm* not *talking about the issues she presents!*

So on what is she actually basing her opinion . . . if *not* on the issues that I present?! How funny is that?? On my grammar? My vocab? The color of my (uncovered) hair???

If there's any depth of hatred it's surely coming from these vitriolic holier-than-thou fanatics. Does she think I hate Danit? Does Danit think that? What, were we supposed to write a 'feel-good' book about loving each other, tra la la la?

Oh dearie dearie me.

Pam x

From: Tzippi Sha-ked (tzippi@connectisra.co.il)
To: Pam Peled (pam-peled@bettaletter.com)
CC: Danit Shemesh (danit.sh@spidimail.co.il)

I don't think there is a depth of hatred coming from the other side – yes, extremist Sikarikim do espouse violence but not the mainstream Haredim . . .

Of course Danit knows you don't hate her and this isn't a 'feel-good' book, but neither is it only about blame. Bottom line, Pam: I wouldn't be here for one extra minute were it not for the Torah wedding me to this land. We *have* to make it work; we have no other choice. Can we coerce the Haredim to do what we want? No. Time will take care of their reality check. I'm more concerned about discourse.

You do understand that I'm coming from a place of much fondness and regard?

Love,

Tzip

From: Pam Peled (pam-peled@bettaletter.com)
To: Tzippi Sha-ked (tzippi@connectisra.co.il)
Danit Shemesh (danit.sh@spidimail.co.il)

Tzip, Danit – I have to make one thing clear:

I DO NOT HATE Haredim

I don't wish them harm, I don't throw dirty diapers at them, I don't mind sitting next to them on a bus or on a plane, or hearing their voices on stage. I wish them well. But I can't condone what they're doing to my society; I can't condone how they impact negatively on the economic and security related issues in Israel, and how they are hysterically mad about gender separation. I feel passionately about it, and my writing reflects my views.

The distortion of Torah is causing too many people to want to divorce the land.

Love you,
Pam x

Email exchanges between Tzippi and Pam:

PAM: You go on and on about respect, Tzip, but respect is a tricky thing. I don't really respect wife-beaters, for example, although I can understand that a terrible childhood can do that to a man. Many Haredim I've encountered have come to their religion through pain – messed up childhoods, drugs, death in the family; I'm not so crash-hot on the transcendental side of it either.

TZIPPI: You can differ from them entirely, but not with an undertone of hatred. Where is this feeling coming from???

PAM: Where does this hatred thing come from? Did I ever use the word? Have you heard of secular people throwing excreta on Haredim? Or spitting at them? Or throwing stones at their cars, burning their trash? Throwing rocks at their policemen – do they even have policemen? Is it *me* who is doing the hating…I don't think so.

From: Tzippi Sha-ked (tzippi@connectisra.co.il)
To: Pam Peled (pam-peled@bettaletter.com),
CC: Danit Shemesh (danit.sh@spidimail.co.il)

A non-Jewish friend weighed in on our discussion. She agreed to share her perspective:

> The sustainability issue proves how different Jewish groups need each other. If everyone was busy protecting Israel's borders, sorting out the finances, doing research and making Judaism "move with the times" to work with the West, just how Jewish would Israel remain?

People would call themselves Jewish – I say I'm Anglican even though all I celebrate is Christmas (and that's only so my tiny family can get together – not exactly religious.)

Yet, if the Haredim ran security and finance, Andorra could invade with a couple of pea-shooters. But they wouldn't want Israel; it would be a poor country with nothing but crowds of studious people.

The two groups have to work together to sustain the country, and recognize each other's contributions.

From: Pam Peled (pam-peled@bettaletter.com)
To: Tzippi Sha-ked (tzippi@connectisra.co.il)
CC: Danit Shemesh (danit.sh@spidimail.co.il)

Dear non-practicing Anglican friend of Tzippi,

Hi. Thank you for your thoughtful email about the necessity of embracing two ways of life in Israel. It's a sweet, romantic sentiment. However, on deeper reflection you will see that this view is patronizing. In order to explain, please seriously consider the following scenario:

Imagine, if you can, an England, where many millions of devout Anglicans lived, largely in their own enclaves (many of which were poverty-stricken.) The men all wear long black coats and big black hats; their women are covered from head to toe. You are expected to dress accordingly, when you enter their areas – say, for example, West Hampstead, or Camden Lock – and if you don't, if you show a shoulder – you might get spat on, or pelted with stones, or have a dirty nappy (and I mean dirty) chucked at you.

There's more: the group of ultra-orthodox Anglicans encourages having large families – eight or nine kids is the norm, but some families have 15 children or more; their demographic strength increases exponentially, and fast.

Most of the men don't work – they study in a church all day; you support them with your hard-earned taxes. You support their children – who also study in church – and who don't study math, or British history, or Shakespeare. Their kids only study Christianity; you, and your kids, support them down the generations, even though they'll soon outnumber you. Because their numbers are growing they're moving into Hampstead

Garden Suburb too, and beyond, where they'd like you to respect their way of life.

If, for example, you use a tube-line in their area, they'd like you to sit at the back (and cover up) – otherwise you might find yourself being shoved, shouted/spat at, or physically hurt. They don't want your daughters to sing in choirs if men are present; they don't want young girls to dance at public openings of new bridges – and Boris Johnson capitulates, or he'll be voted out. They believe that Sunday is a day of rest; they riot in Central London each Sunday against free, open parking lots; they want all Londoners to be in Church, not gallivanting.

They are looking after your spirituality.

Okay. Now, imagine, if you can, that England is still at war with Germany and Italy. It's not a war of 5 years; this war has lasted longer than England's whole existence. You go to the army; you send your kids.

The devout Anglicans don't go to the army; they stay at home in their neighbourhoods, praying for you. You pay for them to stay at home and pray.

Because their many, many kids don't do the army, yours have to enlist for longer; 3 years for boys, 2 for girls. Their boys pray for you. Their girls get married at about 18, and start having babies who'll grow up to pray for you.

In my country this ultra-zealot group is called "Haredi." This is my feeling: they are ultra-something... but I don't think it's Jewish. I don't want them looking after my spirituality. I don't believe Jews should wear long black coats and big black hats – I think that's cultish, not Jewish. If they want to dress in black, or orange, or grow hari-krishna hair, that's okay by me, but why should I pay?

It seems unfair, no?

Oh, I forgot to mention. Those devout Anglicans, living in Camden, largely don't pay taxes if they do work, or parking fines. Some of their leaders run butcheries, say, but feel exempt from income tax (they pray for the country, after all.) If a bunch of London Bobbies enters to demand the tax, or to defuse a suspicious article that might be a bomb, the police might be pelted with rocks and nappies.

And, oh! If the Anglicans feel that other British are behaving badly – let's say organizing a Gay Parade – the devout will come out *en masse* and burn garbage bins all over town. They are protecting you from yourselves.

Seriously, non-practicing Anglican friend of Tzippi, would you be happy?

I'm not happy, like many Israelis, including Tzippi.

Still, I am happy you take Israel's welfare to heart – I hope to welcome you one day into my home and to chat.

Yours,

Pam

From: Tzippi Sha-ked (tzippi@connectisra.co.il)
To: Pam Peled (pam-peled@bettaletter.com)
CC: Danit Shemesh (danit.sh@spidimail.co.il)

Dear Pam:

I agree with much of your email. But: just as Skinheads don't represent secular British society, neither do the nappie-pelting, bin-burning Sikarikim represent Haredim. True, the general inhabitants of Mea She'arim should be condemned for not reining in these monsters.

Haredi society is like spoiled, rebellious, ridiculous teenagers who are out of control. They have a 'holier-than-thou' attitude, and they've been indulged; as a result they don't think clearly. As change comes, (less support from the U.S. post-recession is one factor), they will moderate. When that day comes, we don't want bitter memories of vicious discourse. We want to play to the majority, not to the fringe element. We must offer opportunities, while withholding funding. Our goals can be accomplished in a constructive way.

From: Pam Peled (pam-peled@bettaletter.com)
To: Danit Shemesh (danit.sh@spidimail.co.il)
CC: Tzippi Sha-ked (tzippi@connectisra.co.il)

...just walked in from lunch with one of my closest friends – modern Orthodox...we discussed our project and I realized that her voice is missing. She says she just 'hasn't got the energy' to even consider all these, 'crazy', ideas (her term) – she has 4 *shomrei Shabbat* kids who wear jeans (boys and girls), go to mixed beaches and concerts, and definitely don't keep the laws of *negiah*. Yet they consider themselves totally religious. The no-touching and no-listening to women's voices etc. make her cringe. I feel we need to include this 'normative religious voice' in our book, no?

From: Danit Shemesh (danit.sh@spidimail.co.il)
To: Tzippi Sha-ked (tzippi@connectisra.co.il)
Pam Peled (pam-peled@bettaletter.com)

Hi ladies, here I am, back in the saddle. This is some chapter. Wow, Pam, you are really suffering from us. I am sorry, it is truly uncomfortable to feel that way in your own home. Here you are minding your own business and some 'hairy cowboy' comes into your frame and soils your perfect scene. Yet to paint one group in such a black color is one dimensional and frankly, cheap. You have a fantastic way with words, why use them to separate and stigmatize?

It's all clear for you: the 'hairy cowboys' are to blame, we are the embodiment of evil. That's very helpful because now we can have a movement, raise flags, write articles.

Having said that, I can totally see why you feel the way you do: when you take G-d out of the picture your arguments are valid. That's why we can never see eye-to-eye on this.

You feel sorry for me Pam because I don't joke about sex, but I truly don't comprehend how one can find even an ounce of happiness or inner peace without the G-d component.

Why don't our boys both go to the army *and* learn? What is missing in the world today is *mesirut nefesh* (giving one's all.) It is a totality of being, a directive which guides the young. It's the single most important tool for the odyssey of life. Medical students need it, and high ranking soldiers in the army. Any project worth anything needs *mesirut nefesh*. We wholly believe in this mission, although perhaps you mock it, and we do not compromise.

Compromise is the beginning of dilution; it leads to the breakdown of our belief system. That's what's missing today: potent belief in an ideal. The very idea of doing both army and Torah is testament to a diluted society. Total dedication is the essence of leadership, of accomplishing ideals. Imagine Ghandi fasting for half a week, or Einstein playing for half the day and working on science the other half, or the President quilting for half his time. This is dilution, and purposeless. The only reason for us to spend less time studying would be to appease you folk, you who bash us. This is exactly what the modern orthodox do – appease the secular.

The Haredi community is not good at appeasement. We believe each Jew is a world unto himself and each of us has the power to change the world. To us each boy is a potential Einstein, a potential leader of the Jewish people.

Lots of affection,
Danit

From: Pam Peled (pam-peled@bettaletter.com)
To: Danit Shemesh (danit.sh@spidimail.co.il)
Tzippi Sha-ked (tzippi@connectisra.co.il)

Hello, hello – and lovely to hear from you, Danit… life seems to be never-ending drama these days… how are we going to get through it all? I, for one, want to be old, with a happy, healthy old husband, and happy, healthy oldish kids, and happy, healthy grandchildren and peace on earth and love and laughter for all. And some good coffee, and chocolate. How does that sound?

I fear, Danit, that we will never even agree on the parameters of our differences. I don't want to take God out of the picture. I like having God in the picture – I like God. Do you think Tzippi's family has taken God out of the picture? But her kids (and those in her community) go to university, become productive members of society, and do the army. That is my bottom line. Medical students go to the army; they become army doctors for a time. High ranking soldiers in the army study in Hesder, often. Do Hesder boys represent a 'diluted society?'

Ghandi drank orange juice, and Einstein had hobbies (women, for a kickoff, took up lots of his time). President Peres reads books, Obama plays golf; are they all 'diluted?'

You claim modern orthodox go to the army to appease 'us folk?' I'm not sure that's well-thought out… and this doesn't mean I don't love you!

I think we should move on to the next chapter – we're all starting to repeat ourselves, and hitting a brick wall.

This has been a philosophical evening . . . I'm ready to spend a month on my brother's island in Canada, where the most controversial issue is why Mrs Wooley is building her wall another brick higher . . . *allevai aleinu.*

Laila tov, health, peace, happy family relationships and serenity for all – sweet, sweet dreams . . .

Pam xxx

From: Danit Shemesh (danit.sh@spidimail.co.il)
To: Tzippi Sha-ked (tzippi@connectisra.co.il)
CC: Pam Peled (pam-peled@bettaletter.com)

Pam,

I believe your community and Tzippi's suffer from a sacred cow called 'university.' As a Masters graduate I can tell you that University did not prepare me for life, life did. I paid 'University' my dues and got little in return. Our young people prepare for life when they are ready and not before. They aren't cradled in University, nor do they put off beginning real living and taking on responsibilities. When they begin their life as married people they can attend an array of courses geared to learning specifically what they must know, as opposed to philosophizing and theorizing. Yes, the winds are shifting and more and more Haredim are becoming professionals, on their own terms, on their own conditions, without having to bow to any sacred cow. As far as Gandhi or Einstein, well, they obviously took time off in order to get back to their business at hand; they had breaks, not distractions. The army is directly antithetical to Yeshiva life for our boys, especially when considering the testosterone levels of that age. You cannot do both and stay directed.

Danit.

From: Pam Peled (pam-peled@bettaletter.com)
To: Tzippi Sha-ked (tzippi@connectisra.co.il)
Danit Shemesh (danit.sh@spidimail.co.il)

Did you see the news?

. . . Haredim and *Hassidim* beating each other up in Mea She'arim . . . with iron poles and God knows what – war. Black coats flying in the fray. Take off your wigs, ladies – and slip into something more comfortable like a nice pair of jeans... there is *no holiness* in this type of religion – it's all just a load of $%#@! Now no women can work as guards in Jerusalem???!!! It's out of all control – time for women to stand up, tell these hooligans where to get off – sing as loudly as you can in the presence of those black-hooded hypocrites. Rip off your long skirts!

That's my message: ultra-piousness is not religion; it's a chauvinist plot, madness, and crazy cultish crap.

Don't let them fool you – God has got *nothing* to do with this lot!

Pam xxx

From: Tzippi Sha-ked (tzippi@connectisra.co.il)
To: Pam Peled (pam-peled@bettaletter.com)
CC: Danit Shemesh (danit.sh@spidimail.co.il)

Yes, this country is going to pot! Meanwhile, I'll 'skirt' the issue...

From: Pam Peled (pam-peled@bettaletter.com)
To: Tzippi Sha-ked (tzippi@connectisra.co.il)
Danit Shemesh (danit.sh@spidimail.co.il)

Hi Tzippi and Danit – Stop Press: Meuchedet Health Clinic printed a booklet on breast cancer. Because of religious sensibilities they couldn't use the word 'breast.' They had to say "the special woman's cancer," which is not even factual – men get... wait for the word... *breast* cancer (shhhhhhh!!!) as well.

It's your *yishuv*'s living room all over again – hysterical puritanicalism gone mad – and *nothing, nothing, nothing* to do with God, religion or Judaism itself. Poor, poor Israel – it's going to collapse over this... mark my words.

So – to shower, to wash my special woman's organs, to prepare lessons, and to write my next chapter. Not sure if I can even show it to you – you might throw me out of the country... and, you know what... I might just thank you. Really – we are passing the boundaries of sanity here.

Oh my. Where is God when we need him most... why doesn't He knock some sense into His 'followers?'

Love and hugs – from my tainted, uncovered arms,
Pam xxx

From: Tzippi Sha-ked (tzippi@connectisra.co.il)
To: Pam Peled (pam-peled@bettaletter.com)

Dear Pam, I've reread our book and feel you've failed to examine how secular/Reform/Conservative Judaism can sustain the Jewish nation. I take no joy quoting the results of the recent Pew Commission regarding the status of American Jewry in November of 2013. Here's what Daniel Gordis had to say:

> "But one fundamental conclusion is inescapable: The massive injection of capital into the post-1990 study "continuity" agenda has failed miserably. Non-Orthodox Judaism is simply disappearing in America. Judaism has long been a predominantly content-driven, rather than a faith-driven enterprise, but we now have a generation of Jews secularly successful and well-educated, but so Jewishly illiterate that nothing remains to bind them to their community or even to a sense that they hail from something worth preserving. By abandoning a commitment to Jewish substance, American Jewish leaders destroyed the very enterprise they claimed to be preserving.
>
> Nowhere is this rapid collapse more visible than in the Conservative movement, which is practically imploding before our eyes".
>
> (Jewish Review of Books *"Conservative Judaism: A Requiem"* by Daniel Gordis | Winter 2014)

The Reform and Conservative movements are dead. What now, Pam? Oblivion? As for your vibrant secular Tel Aviv culture, once it's exported abroad there is this to report:

> "Numerous studies have found that secular Israelis living abroad find it difficult to pass on their specifically Israeli identity to their children. That was one of the conclusions reached by Prof. Lilach Lev Ari, head of the Oranim Academic College of Education's sociology department, in her book "Israeli Americans: Migration, Transnationalism and Diasporic Identity," authored together with Prof. Uzi Rebhun.

Apparently, an identity built solely on Israeliness is not very durable in the Diaspora."

(Israeliness and Assimilation, *Jerusalem Post* Nov. 13, 2013)

Well, well. The only viable alternative for Israel seems to be observant halachic Judaism – either Modern or Hardal. Enough said.

– Tzippi

Chapter Nine

Mental Hygiene for the Jewish Soul: A Prescription from Three Maidels

Danit writes:

THE LAST CHAPTER

Can we possibly understand each other? Do we truly hate one other? Are we terrified of the 'other'? Can we come together? No, no, no, and yes. I am in a unique position to answer because, at the risk of sounding like Dr. Seuss, I have been where Pamela is, and I have thought of joining Tzippi where she is, and here I am, where I am. While I can't say the Haredi system is perfect, it's the most intellectually honest of the three. Yes, human frailty has seeped into the system and we have our fanatics who will not stop making waves. Yes, we are politically incorrect and downright unseemly in appearance, according to your aesthetic preferences. I also agree that the pure written law has been misunderstood and taken out of proportion by extremists, whom we disdain.

I will share our recipe: We hold fast to simplicity in this convoluted world, and stick to Torah as our guiding light. We are Haredim *le dvar Hashem*: our axis of existence rests on faith that:

a) G-d exists
b) He gave us the Torah
c) He loves us and acts like a loving father
d) We are obligated to His Torah
e) There exists an absolute, a formula, to living well

Each generation does not have to reinvent the wheel, making up laws as they go. We lean on the ancient word as Truth, and don't sway a millimeter lest we lose our footing. A hierarchy of wise men understand the written word; there is very little guesswork in our system, which helps us stay directed and potent. Our main aim is to become better persons in the eyes of G-d. Our priorities are clear and we fight with gumption to protect the 'profound': the Shabbat, women, marriage etc.; we place the 'profane' in second place.

The word 'ultra-orthodox' is divisive. We don't refer to ourselves as 'ultra,' we are simply Jews. Throughout history devout Jews always abided by a standard of behavior without less stringent Jews stigmatizing them as primitive, or separate. It is not we who changed the rules of the game. We remain the original version of our nation.

The Hardalim or Leumim are inspired and motivated. Their axis is anchored in the principle that this land is our land and we can have it all: Torah and modernity and cutting-edge education. Perhaps, Tzippi, your voice is the most rational. You truly despise fanaticism. When your non-Jewish friend wrote with calm understanding of all sides, Pamela questioned her authority. You know why? Because, Tzippi, you can't have a foot in both worlds. Your group *suffers* from 'the holy trinity': Torah, work, and the land. No-one knows which is most important, so all become crucial. This is problematic when a choice is necessary: which *is* more important and *who is* to say? Back in HaRav Kook's time, perhaps it was possible to live simultaneously in both the material and spiritual worlds. Today, it isn't – life is too dichotomized.

The secular are loud and proud survivalists. Their flirtation with anarchy and their notion that there is no G-d is, on a foundational level, repulsive to us. Their sheer chutzpa of negating the obvious just to enjoy 'freedom' stuns us. The word *Chilonim* comes from the word *chol*, the opposite of *kadosh*, it means 'banal' as opposed to 'sublime.' They emphasize the *chol*, the material, as opposed to *kodesh,* the spiritual existence, and they're as extreme as the Haredim. If anything, Pam, we are more alike than not, only on different sides of the continuum. I only wish I knew what you stand *for*, rather than what you stand *against*. I know well the reactionary, fear-based slogans vis-à-vis the Haredim and the Hardalim. What I don't know is what you love, what you fight for; what is your *ani maamin*? Is it the freedom to wear bikinis? Is it freedom of speech? It can't be the latter; as soon as a bearded man speaks you yell at him to shut up. Is it about placing women center stage? But your women so often complain of harassment, denigration and misunderstanding. Is your goal to be like the goyim?

At the end of the day, can we understand each other? Perhaps not.

Do we hate each other?

This is the Haredi perspective: we feel our garb and appearance are ridiculed, our children considered pathetic, and our lunatics misconstrued as the norm. We are accosted by huge billboards of almost naked women advertising bikinis; planted, most inappropriately, in our neighborhoods. The general consensus is that "we are the ones you love to hate." That is made crystal clear by the media. 'Experts,' from psychologists to babysitters, are polled for opinions of the Haredi community. The Secular love ex-Haredim, those who were once insiders and have now 'sensibly' left the fold, free of our chains.

As for us: we do not hate you. We are different, but harbor no hatred for the secular. Pluralistic families, containing all the different *hashkafot* of the rainbow, survive well enough. If each one is evolved in their person-hood, they all remain loving. It's when a post-Haredi badmouths his roots that the media preys on him.

Any aware secular person, even if intravenously hooked to the news, must realize how the media pounce on and lynch us. Talk about thinking for yourself, Pamela! Do you really believe that most Haredim go around spitting on little girls? Most of them have little girls of their own. (By the way, when a secular man spat on a Haredi teenage girl and she reported it to the media, they wouldn't print the story.) If you were the mother of that eight-year-old who was harassed by a name-calling Haredi, would you use her as a poster child to vilify the Haredim? That little girl has been branded as "the one who was spat upon." The PC mother says on camera that harassment must be stopped, while her poor little girl sits in the corner, embarrassed. Could the greater transgression be using a child for political gain? Remember: we're talking about a single madman, not a daily phenomenon. Sure there are wars, but why place your children on the front lines...?

As for the nonsense about the buses...so much tax money spent on informing the public to report whether women are asked to move to the back of the bus. How many times a day is a woman asked to move? The two recent incidents were plastered endlessly in all the papers, making the phenomenon seem greater than it is.

The sign on the bus should actually state: 'No accidental rubbing up against girls/women,' or 'no whistling, cajoling, or uninvited flirting.' I think it's *women* who want to sit separately, and for good reason. I know you'll accuse me of being astoundingly 'chauvinistic,' but the ugly truth is females constantly complain about being accosted on buses.

At the end of the day, each Jew will realize that the media is a circus. Deep down, each of us knows we have to accept 'the other,' and that acceptance is the first step to love. Our Jewish essence is love: *ve'ahavta lere'acha kamocha.*

Are we terrified of each other?

Recently, an ex-Mossad leader declared the Haredim more dangerous to Israel than Iranian nuclear weapons. This is terror-mongering at its best, and the media seizes such opportunities. They gleefully report on a couple of religious soldiers who excuse themselves while a female singer performs, an old man who continues to walk even as the *tzphira* (memorial siren) reminds us of fallen Jewish soldiers, and a man who stops a bus to protest a woman sitting behind the driver. The grievance list is long, I know, but it isn't an issue for me. Every community has a list of faults. Blazing them onto headlines is more disturbing. It's like selling rotten tomatoes to throw at apes in the zoo.

To fear numbers on charts and virtual statistics, no matter how convincing, is simplistic at best, and paranoid at worse. For every study you bring proving we are dangerous parasites, I can bring two proving you are steering us towards destruction. It's a barren exercise in futility. Yes, our numbers are growing and might change the face of Israel, but if you got to know us, you would find that we are not the enemy. We are an integral part of you. Furthermore, we make sure Jews are still recognizable as Jews.

Your obsessive compulsion to denigrate Haredim proves that you define yourself by who you are not. The fact that we're diametrically opposed to your approach to life shocks you. The sight of us frightens you, the thought that your daughter could one day look like *that* keeps you up at night. So you objectify us till we're no longer human; we become 'parasites' and 'a burden on society.' It's a cheap trick and it works... temporarily. Still, I ask myself if your fear is legitimate or merely your own full-blown identity crisis.

So, can we come together? We *are* together. We *can* all live here and we *do* all live here. This G-d given land is meant for all of us. We are organs, sinews, bones of the same body. The entire body suffers when the tip of the little finger hurts. We can count on *Eretz Israel* to contain contradictions, and even thrive on them. Each of us has a role to play, one for which we are best suited. Differing points of view are not frightening in and of themselves. On the contrary, that we disagree is one of the few constants in our precarious existence. What is frightening is that both your community and mine are beginning to pontificate that neither can thrive, so long as the other exists. Can a brain ostracize a heart because it cannot understand it?

We are all on the same ship, each in our own compartment, heading in the same direction. Whether we like it or not, we're in this together. Those in one compartment may believe that those in another are drilling a hole in the ship. Needless to say, if so we would all drown. But in truth, G-d is in charge of the ship. Thank goodness no flesh and blood human has any real power. Haredim do not make distinctions; we accept all Jews as fellow passengers. How we arrive at our destination, even if the other is drilling a perceived hole, is not our business. It's G-d's business, His department. We're terrified only when G-d is out of the picture. Then people become dangerous as they stew in their own convictions established to serve a hedonistic need for 'freedom.'

The people we love as brethren; it's their behavior we disdain.

We all live in confusion and chaos; the ship tosses about in a storm. The Unknown looms overhead, ridiculing us. None of us know how to struggle with the unknown ahead. The secular create philosophies on how to live, while spreading fear about extremists who don't abide by these theories. The *leumim* can't decide what religious tenet to loosen and what to enforce more strictly, as they try to appease the secular. The Haredim remain what they always have been: believers.

As the old joke goes: a Rabbi tried to negotiate peace between two warring parties. He heard each side as he stroked his beard, deep in thought. To the first he simply said, 'you are right.' To the other side he announced, 'and you are right.' Both parties exclaimed, dumbfounded, 'but we can't both be right!' To that the Rabbi responded simply, 'you are right again.'

Writing this book has been both joyful and painful. I thank both you ladies for giving me an experience I will not forget. My sincere prayer is that each of us will remember that we are Jews first and foremost, and then decide how we each want to manifest that, without hating *The Other.*

From: Pam Peled (pam-peled@bettaletter.com)
To: Danit Shemesh (danit.sh@spidimail.co.il)
CC: Tzippi Sha-ked (tzippi@connectisra.co.il)

Danit – just read your chapter, and I feel your pain. I'm truly sorry if I implied that all Haredim spit on little girls. However, having said that, more and more Haredim themselves are questioning where the 'moderate' voices are – where is the public condemnation of craziness by Haredi leaders? So, it's more complicated.

Our fear of the Haredism or Iranism of Israel is not really about the spitters and the bus-bullies; it's about the whole unsustainability of the system...and I wish you would relate to that. Show me the studies you say you can produce that counter my statistics – I'd be tremendously interested to read them, and fabulously relieved to be proven wrong.

I am working, in my chapter, to produce real solutions to the terrible rifts in our society – we simply *have* to end on a note of *'piyus'* and understanding. I am thinking of real and practical solutions here – not simply words like 'we don't hate each other; we need to accept each other.' What can *actually*, practically, be done?

Somehow, somewhere, sometimes, I just get that feeling that deep, deep, deep down in your gorgeous heart and body there is this spirit wishing to kick off her shoes and walk bare-feet on the beach and yes, maybe even have a dip in the ocean in a bathing suit, with men and women and babies all splashing around and having a wonderful time...no? Maybe it's just wishful thinking on my part...for all I know you might fantasize that I'd like to don a wig and cover my elbows... and, you know what... maybe I do.

And then, again, maybe not.

Too late at night – I just type nonsense at this hour – tell me to go to bed...

Shavua tov, again, and hugs,

Pam x

From: Danit Shemesh (danit.sh@spidimail.co.il)
To: Pam Peled (pam-peled@bettaletter.com)
CC: Tzippi Sha-ked (tzippi@connectisra.co.il)

It is written in the Torah, '...and you shall love your neighbor as you do yourself.' Rabbi Akiva said this was *'klal gadol ba Torah'*; the principal message of the Torah. It assumes that one loves first oneself, which gives a point of reference as to how to love the other. We can infer that if one does not know how to love others, perhaps one suffers from a lack of self-love. Self-love leads to loving others, as opposed to hating them. Of course, I don't mean inflated ego and pride. I mean true love which only comes from a deep understanding that we're all G-d's creations. Hating the other would be like hating my best friend's child, only on a much, much grander scale, and would ultimately pervert my view of myself. You see, we are all connected in an intricate and beautiful web.

In *Pirkei Avot*, Rabbi Eliezer says, 'one should esteem one's friend on the same level as one esteems oneself.' Ben Zoma adds, 'who is honored? He who honors others.' How true that is. There are feared people, loved people, and appreciated people. We tend to appreciate those who appreciate us, irrespective of their social standing. Human beings appreciate connection; animosity only serves to ostracize people and escalate problems.

So, Pam, I hold fast to my solution. Each of us contributes something to the nation of Israel. Your sector contributes the work force and the army. Tzippi's sector contributes the love of the land, and passion. Our contribution is the uncompromising stronghold on G-d's word, the very purpose in life. Hating us because you don't understand our contribution is like the right hand hating the left for not being the same. What truly hurts you is your hatred, not us.

Of the three of us, I believe I am most equipped to love you as my neighbor, as I'm commanded to do so. You both sway in the winds of change, affected by headlines. It's an unstable *hashkafa* and renders you fickle. Yet, no matter what you say, I see you as an integral part of the fabric.

From: Danit Shemesh (danit.sh@spidimail.co.il)
To: Pam Peled (pam-peled@bettaletter.com)
CC: Tzippi Sha-ked (tzippi@connectisra.co.il)

Hi Pamela, I have to share with you some additional thoughts: I'm the only one unpublished of the three of us and I have felt daunted by the idea of writing with you both, but I kept going anyway. Countless times I've rethought whether or not to go on, as I don't want my writing to fall short and not get my point across as well as you do. Even though I don't represent the Haredi community, I am Haredi.

The reason I kept going is that I have a unique vantage point, being a *baal teshuva* and having had my own struggles. A *baal teshuva* harbors the secular self inside even after she's changed her behaviors and attitudes. There's still that secular being who would agree with what you say about freedom. Of course I want to run down the beach barefoot with hair flying. Every time I get that urge I introspect for just a minute, and remind myself anew why I made this move; the payback is tremendous, but the price is expensive. You see the price but not the payback, because your perspective is not my experience.

This project has helped sharpen the reasons for my 'transfer.' You raised good points to which I gave serious thought, and I now realize that I'm willing to pay the price of bikinis and walks on the beach hand-in-hand with my husband in order to fit into a community which is not always user-friendly. At the end of the day, I feel more at home now than any place I have ever lived, and I have globe-trotted. I feel accepted, welcomed and secure.

It took the project to show me that questions, even those for which I have no answers, are parenthetical to the heart of the matter: the Haredi community is authentic and humane, with keen foresight. Perhaps I kept writing through my internal crises because the friction helped me realize I am where I belong. Please read my words at face value, and don't just think I'm rationalizing to myself. Trust me when I say, I am a good consumer of communities. I have run the gamut.

Sincerely,

Danit

Pam Writes:

MY TAKE:

Jews have not had an easy ride in Vienna. In 1420 they comprised five percent of the city, until Duke Albrecht V confiscated their property, destroyed their *shul*, and kicked them out. Some decades later they were allowed to return, chucked out again in 1669, and then asked to come back when Vienna's economy crumbled. Periods of calm were punctured by bouts of anti-Semitism until 1841 when a Jewish renaissance began – a golden period for Austrian Jews, who flourished until the beginning of World War II. Sigmund Freud was Austrian, and Martin Buber; Theodor Herzl, Max Nordau, Gustav Mahler, and Franz Kafka. Three out of four Austrian Nobel Prize winners for medicine were Jews, and more than half the doctors, dentists, and lawyers were Jewish too.

In Vienna's only synagogue that escaped the ravages of WWII, there is a plaque for Jews who died fighting for Austria in WWI. Next to it is a huge stone book, its granite leaves engraved with the 65,000 names of Austrian Jews murdered in the Holocaust. Next to that is another plague, with the almost 200 names of survivors of Auschwitz and Birkenau who came to Israel, and died fighting in the War of Independence.

On a frosty Friday night at the end of 2011, I was one of about eight women sitting upstairs in the ornate synagogue, in a gallery that could hold hundreds. I looked down at the men below; mostly old, and not too many even of them, and the sad, strange history of the Jews hit me hard. I had left my glasses in the hotel, the words of the *siddur* swam in front of my eyes, and the tunes were mostly different from those I knew. I prayed and I cried, and prayed and cried some more, my tears flowing freely as I watched my husband below me with the men – frail and so very ill, as he bravely swayed and sang, despite the cancer eating up his body. As I dripped mascara onto the wooden pews, I thought for long minutes about *Three Ladies, Three Lattes,* and the ungodly mess we are making of our blessed homeland, after all our troubles and travails. And this time it's *us* that are doing it to us; we ourselves are becoming our own worst enemy.

And I thought to myself: this has got to stop.

I, too, am much to blame for what Tzippi calls the 'harsh and cutting rhetoric.' On the plane to Vienna I had occasion to look out for a Haredi rabbi, who had offered to host us for Shabbat dinner. I am ashamed to admit that as I approached the few Haredi men on the flight and asked their names, I was filled with what comes close to revulsion. It's not just how uncouth they looked to me: wild hair flying, unwieldy clothes, and so many packages; it's what they stand for, and the issues that I associate with them. Suddenly I felt revulsion for myself as I realized with a thump a terrible truth: I am becoming anti-Semitic. It's not anti-'Semitic,' of course; I'm not anti-Jews. But I fear that I'm falling into an abyss of being anti-what I call the 'cultist' Jews – the competitive *kashrut* keepers, the black-coated, *Shabbos* fanatics. 'Anti-Semultist,' I could say, or 'anti-Cultimitic.' Whatever it is, it's a more than shocking thing – and one that I'm hearing repeated all over town. "I'm becoming anti-Semitic," say my friends, and many who aren't my friends; that's evolving, inevitably, into "I hate them."

What is happening to the Jews?

It's not "them," as such; it's not Danit. It's not my cousins, who live in some black area of Jerusalem, (to their secular family's dismay); it's not my teacher from Beit Vegan. It's what the amorphous "they" are doing to Israel, and it's not all of them. I know it's the *Sikarikim*, the *Neturai Karta*, the *Toldot Aharon* extremist minority. I know that the vast majority of Haredim are peace-loving and don't spit at little girls for showing an elbow, or shove women from the front of the bus. I know that. But I'm caught up in the maelstrom of emotions that fly so fast in this crowded corner of the world, and I can't help myself.

But I have to help myself. I have to rise above this gut reaction, and find some way of compromise and co-existence. So I turned to the college students whom I teach, the future leaders of secular Israel, (though some are Modern Orthodox too), and asked for a prescription for peace. "Let them take off their uniforms and join the army," was the overwhelming reaction, "and go to work. Let them pay their taxes, and learn maths and science, and roll up their sleeves and become productive members of society. Let them stop living off my income tax. Then we can talk acceptance."

So how do we do that?

It's complicated. First of all, we have to build a big wall. Not between the ultra-religious and the less so, but between religion itself, and the state. *No more handouts* because you wear black hats. No more rabbis deciding who can and can't get married, who can be buried where, what conditions must be met for divorce. Religion stays in the home, and in the synagogue; politics and religion do not mix. Everyone has equal rights and equal responsibilities: the same military service, the same taxes, the same working for a living. Immediately the feeling of being a '*freir*' (a fool) for carrying so many burdens on our backs will evaporate, and the ante will be downed, not upped.

We need a more integrated society; without enclaves of Haredim or Hardalim. Just like the Modern Orthodox and the secular live together in apartment blocks in Ra'anana and Modi'in, so should the zealots live among the people of Israel. Now I'm not at all sure I'd like to live next door to the perfectly pious; in fact I most certainly wouldn't, but I think it's the only way. In your house you can praise God however you like, eat what you like, wear what you like; in the streets religion is not up for discussion. Yes, it'll take some adjusting for the devout to see girls dressed less decorously than those wrapped in yards of fabric from head to toe, but they'll have to get used to it. If they truly believe in their way, nothing should threaten them. And yes, it'll be weird for me to live cheek by jowl with a culture that is foreign; but maybe I'll get to know them over a borrowed box of (kosher) milk, and we'll have a (kosher) coffee with that milk, and I'll discover that many religious 'nuts' are just like Danit, and not loony at all.

My husband thinks our kids should study together, in egalitarian schools, and learn to know and understand each other's hearts. In the morning all pupils will learn the core curriculum: history, and maths, and English, and Science. In the afternoon each can choose tennis or a talmud *chug,* study *Gemara* or Genetics. Or even both.

I harbor hopes for Israel. I wish my black-garbed brethren would loosen up a little, and adapt to the Middle Eastern sun. I'd like to see them in jeans, or at least daring to expose a toe inside a sandal on a hot, hot day...maybe then I'd cover up my cleavage in the (mixed) supermarket down the road, so as not to lure any stray *Haredi* into wanton thoughts of wickedness. (I don't usually display much cleavage, and I'm presumably past the age of eliciting wanton thoughts, but you get my drift.) Just as brown-haired Jews live peaceably among the blond, and slim Jews and plump coexist with the tall and the short, so should the less and more religiously inclined share the same air.

I will start with myself. As of today, I will try to quash feelings of negativity when I see black beards, or gray ones, under big black hats, or unshapely women in corduroy skirts and berets. I will remind myself that we are all people trying to make sense of the world, and trying to live in it as best we can. I will think of Danit, and of Tzippi, and of sipping large lattes in the living room together with sweet pastries in hand...and I will work on myself to be more accepting of 'the other.'

It won't be simple. But it has to be done.

Here is the essential, indispensable ingredient that our world needs now: humor. We need to learn to laugh at ourselves – laugh, and roar, and hold our bellies, doubled over until we ache. We need to laugh at 'the other' – but also to chuckle at our own idiosyncrasies, and admit that we may be a bit over the top. In a marriage, when each partner can laugh at their own mistakes and move on, the marriage flows and love grows. Where there's intransigence, and stubborn sticking to the *my-viewpoint-right-or-wrong*, there's trouble ahead. Let's laugh at ourselves, loudly – and make music and make love (not necessarily with each other – and certainly not before we're married...although, wait a minute...might that not be the mother-of-all-solutions?)

Here's to peace, and love; joy, health and laugher, in a sane and boring world.

Amen.

P.S. Stop press! It seems as if there really is a God. I finished typing this chapter and got up to have dinner with my family, and then to watch TV. Lo and behold – on the nine o' clock news, an item: *Kibbutz Shluchot* (a religious kibbutz in the Beit She'an Valley) and it's neighbor *Kibbutz*

Reshafim (a secular kibbutz next door) are building a communal hamlet between the two, called *Shlafim.* It's designed for secular, religious, and even 'mixed' couples – where, believe it or not – the wife keeps Shabbat and the husband doesn't, or vice versa. "We don't have a 'datometer' (religious measurement device)," explains one of the organizers, "we accept whoever wants to be part of our egalitarian way of life." And yes, there are fears, on both sides. Religious kibbutzniks worry that their members might 'slip' from the road, and nip into the secular kibbutz on Shabbat, for a swim. The secular surely harbor fears too, of an encroaching religious presence. But, they say, "we have all been good friends for years and years; the time has come to live together."

Whew. A case of serendipity as I write my final words? I usually watch the eight o' clock news, and, had dinner not been delayed tonight by my brother and his wife dropping by to share an anniversary *lechaim*, I would have missed this story.

Or is there a guiding hand letting me know just as I wrap up this 16 month project that yes! There is a middle way... and we had jolly well learn to walk the walk.

I think I believe in the Hand.

My hand may be at the end of a naked, tanned arm, and yours might be clad in a long, clinging sleeve... but I extend mine to you, in friendship. In fact, I open my bare arms to you, in the hope of a hug.

Please hug me back.

From: Danit Shemesh (danit.sh@spidimail.co.il)
To: Pam Peled (pam-peled@bettaletter.com)

Pam, do you really expect a *'kol hakavod'* for making some of your best friends Haredim? You would force situations that are impossible, just to fit your Pleasantville scene. Perhaps you are a magical thinker, but I'm more of a realist. And I'm not different from others in my world. I am Haredi and proud of it. Your superficial outlook towards us is your worst enemy; we ourselves are not that enemy. The difference between you and me is that I don't see you as a danger, because I'm plugged into G-d. I know He will redeem us. You will not stop that. I don't hate, because I am commanded against it. In fact, I am commanded to love you. I do not busy myself with your complaints; they are meaningless to me. They don't change my way of life. The only thing left to do is to make sure Israel doesn't lose its Jewish status quo to your politically 'pretty in pink' picture. For this, we need unpopular measures like forcing buses to stop on Shabbat. Yet, I still believe the only way is to accept the 'other' as a part and parcel of the Israeli face. Not to plaster make-up on pock marks.

From: Tzippi Sha-ked (tzippi@connectisra.co.il)
To: Pam Peled (pam-peled@bettaletter.com)
CC: Danit Shemesh (danit.sh@spidimail.co.il)

Hi there! Whew! We did it . . . you did it. . . . the last chapter . . . yours, Pam, somehow sprouted an olive branch and did the job. I liked it very much. As I read "My hand may be at the end of a naked, tanned arm, and yours might be clad in a long, clinging sleeve . . . but I extend mine to you, in friendship" I almost have to ask whether your left hand knew what your right hand was writing?

Tzippi writes:

> *"Kol Yisrael arevim zeh bazeh: All of Israel are responsible for each other"*
>
> The Talmud (Shevuot 39a)

Also:

> *"There is nothing that a good chicken soup can't cure"*

A SEAT IN THE MIDDLE AISLE

Has this project influenced me in any constructive manner? I think so. Each Wednesday I attend my 'Marriage and Family Relations' course in Jerusalem, for religious women. I signed up to try and make a difference in Haredi circles. About two months ago, I walked into a Givat Shaul classroom and found a seat in the center aisle. My choice of chair might not have been subconscious. I sit alongside Modern Orthodox, Chassidish, Litvish, and other Haredi women. As we learn skills to become effective marriage counselors, it dawns on me that this same paradigm could reconcile our fractured nation. Our people must undergo collective marriage counseling because, for better or worse, we are wedded to each other, if not by faith then, as Soloveitchik noted, by fate. But we are all flying 'solo' at the moment.

So here is this *maidel's* prescription for promoting national marital unity and harmony, based on psychoanalytic principles and Cognitive Behavior Therapy (CBT):

NATIONAL GOALS:

- Connecting: Building trust by helping one another help him/herself. (The Haredim could help the secular understand what it means to be Jewish; the secular could teach Haredim professional skills)
- All acknowledging the problem as a collective one (we share a common destiny and fate)
- Monitoring our internal statements about the other
- Labeling behaviors, not people
- Understanding that a relationship is enhanced via talking and sharing

THE THERAPEUTIC PROCESS:

- Identifying our own strengths as well as the other's
- Learning to compliment the other
- Problem solving: applying strengths to overcome mutual problems
- Moving the problem from the emotional to the intellectual realm
- Asking: How does vilifying the other serve us?
- Seeking self-expansion through the successes of the other

I'd like to think we three Maidels can exhale and remain good friends. The truth is that I can't imagine our families sitting down to a calm Shabbat dinner without emotional fireworks desecrating the atmosphere. I can hear Pamela moaning that her food is not glatt, glatter, glattest enough and Danit predicting that Pamela will show up in a bikini, (and she can get away with it,) to underscore her point.

So, I'm not sure we broadened one another as much as we 'branded' each other. And to what end? What was the point of the endless berating? Why gloat when one sector of our nation makes national/international headlines that confirm our paranoia? Granted, our project did allow a certain fleshing out (and flushing out) of our religious coordinates, a 'soul' accounting of where we're heading, but not *yet* a plan of action.

Shame. I did think that we might actually hear one another.

I remember my earlier thought of a boxing ring with two redheads, seeing red, RED, *RED*. I've been less a referee than a spectator, though to Pam I'm part of a puritanical trend. The rhetoric has been harsh and cutting. Pam's corner dripped with facts, figures, and jabs at Haredim. Danit's corner, always wrong to Pam, put up a valiant, if misguided fight, wholly disregarding those same facts and figures, crying that G-d will sort things out. The gaps are wider than can possibly be bridged. So how do we come back from this precipice of failure? For such a 'clever' nation we seem pretty dumb.

We are back at the Tower of Babel, speaking two different languages: one G-d centered, the other decidedly not. Can there be a bridge between those that subscribe to tradition and those that proscribe change? It seems not – the secular are more and more detached from their Jewish moorings, the Haredim more mentally and psychologically paralyzed in theirs. It will take Solomonic wisdom to navigate our waters. I don't have any more answers than when we first started our project. Do you Pam? Danit? Pam, you've presented your case against Haredi society while also casting aspersions against the Modern Orthodox. So who, pray tell, is left practicing Judaism sensibly? I think that you're simply not receptive or tolerant of any positions that go against your precise blend of Judaism. The quality of our shared national life is obviously influenced by our civic engagement (or, in our case, lack thereof.)

As we light the fifth Hanukka candle, I think how without preserving, cherishing and living the Torah, we Jews are finished. How tragic that so many of our brethren have lost their Jewish compass. Pam celebrates Israel's material accomplishments (medical, cultural, technological) rather than its unique Torah heritage. Yet, a Jewish nation, based predominantly on material accomplishments, is an oxymoron. G-d created *this* nation in order to proclaim *His* Glory. The deal is that he won't grant us any peace of mind or freedom from wars until we recognize its raison d'être. This doesn't mean reciting *tehillim* ad infinitum in praise of G-d, but a recognition that He trumps everything else in our daily lives; our mission entails inviting Him into our lives every day and carrying out His will.

Maybe the real problem is that this is plain inconvenient. As R. Feldman notes in his provocative book, *The Eye of the Storm*, "The struggle of human history is the struggle over whether the glory of God or the glory of man will reign supreme."* This was the epicenter of Adam's struggle, and of Yaakov and Esau's, the crux of the war between Rome and the Jews, the reason for the destruction of the Temple as Jews sought to maintain Torah in the face of other nations, and the story of Hanukka. He continues, "The Sages foresaw... that throughout history most of mankind would pursue the path of self-glorification – the antithesis... of the glorification of God... Man, empowered and enamored of his own glory, would turn away completely from pursuing the glory of God."

Secular Zionism is living that description to a fault, while some Modern Orthodox Zionists are turning the land of Israel into a false G-d. Then there are the anti-Zionist Jews that turn Torah into a cult. Just thinking about this makes me fatigued. I think about packing up and leaving too, Pam. I just don't know to where....

To say that we are living in tumultuous times is an understatement. A fascinating *Baraisa*,** describes the pre–Mashiach era:

> In the (Days of the) footsteps of Mashiach, audacity will triumph; prices will soar; the vineyards will be fruitful, yet wine will be expensive.
>
> The government will turn to heresy; there will be no rebuke; the assembly places of the wise will turn to immorality.
>
> The Galil will be destroyed; the Givlan will be desolate; the border dwellers will wander from city to city and will not be pitied.
>
> The wisdom of Torah scholars will be repulsive; those who fear sin will be abominated; truth will be absent.
>
> The young will mortify elders; elders will stand (in respect) before

* HaRav Feldman, A. '*The Footsteps of Mashiach*,' The Eye of the Storm: A Calm View of Raging Issues. Yad Yosef Publications, Jerusalem 2009. p. 168

** Sotah 49b, Sanhedrin 97a, *Derech Eretz Zuta* 10:1

children; a son will humiliate his father; a daughter will rebel against her mother, a daughter-in-law against her mother-in-law.

One's enemies will be his own family; the face of the generation will be the face of a dog; a son will be ashamed of his father.

And upon whom may we rely? Upon our Father in Heaven.*

Pretty heavy stuff, right?

So here we are, wrapping up the project we started before last Hanukka – a festival commemorating how Greek culture failed to obliterate ancient Jews. With what chutzpa, those intransigent Maccabees refused to succumb! Are modern day Hellenists our fellow secular Jews?

On this Festival of Lights, what are you celebrating tonight, Danit? And you, Pam?

We spent a year being cyber-space *kibitzers* and meeting for lattes; we walk away a few calories heavier and emotionally gridlocked. (At least the lattes were good and the ladies lovely.) If our goal was to air our gripes in a constructive manner, I am almost sure we failed. If it was to move forward – *no* to that. Perhaps we did clarify our intransigent positions – yikes, not what I had hoped for!

I, for one, am tired of arguing with the two of you. There are too many front row seats in Israel for the drama of hurtful rhetoric. Statistically, we are up a creek without paddles. One of you will argue that there are no paddles, the other will say that the only paddles are God propelled. I say, forget about the paddles; we're on a flimsy canoe together. We have to deal. I'm bringing up my children in the Holy Land, yes, but also in a strife-filled land. I'm concerned about my children living in a country full of hate. I even hear children (my own included) debating whether Israel has a future. Do kids in America, South Africa, and Europe talk like this?

By offering no solutions we're shortchanging one another. Robert Putnam, political scientist and Harvard Professor of Public Policy, posits that the condition for effective democracy is to promote a culture of

* Harav Feldman, A., *The Footsteps of the Mashiach.* Jerusalem: Yad Yosef Publications, 2009. p. 166.

trust and cooperation, or "*Social Capitol*."* Without it, a democratic political system does not efficiently achieve its goals. Can we ever speak the same language and be mindful of others' sensitivities? Here I would welcome some separation between religion and state, in order to inspire towards Judaism rather than legislate it.

I worry about existentialist threats and cataclysmic events; our fundamental problem is clearly more than simply Fundamentalists. Yet, despite all this, I am encouraged. In our circles the Mashiach is often discussed. When my husband and I signed the lease to our first rental, we were amused by a stipulation: our landlord insisted that if Mashiach arrived, we would need to move out so his family could come home from Brazil. David modified the wording so 'Mashiach' was recognized by both parties. Our landlord agreed that if Mashiach arrived, both families could live in the house together.

Imagine that. *Walla*, we resolved our differences. Perhaps this divided nation can agree that until Mashiach arrives we will abide by democratic rule. When he comes, we will *gladly* revert to the Torah mandate.

Makes sense to me ladies.

From: Pam Peled (pam-peled@bettaletter.com)
To: Tzippi Sha-ked (tzippi@connectisra.co.il)
Danit Shemesh (danit.sh@spidimail.co.il)

As always, I find Tzippi's voice calm, adult, caring, and nurturing. I agree: the three of us can remain good friends – for sure.

Point of interest: I don't wear bikinis (not anymore, not for years and years and years. My girls all do, and look stunning; *kein yirbu*!)

You are wrong, of course, about secular society – Chaucer was secular, Michaelangelo was secular, Shakespeare and James Joyce and the Beatles were secular – do you think they had no finger on the pulse of ideals and philosophy and spirituality? Is it 'spiritual' to beg for money for chicken on Fri. for your kids, because you're so blessedly poor that you can't afford to buy it yourself? Where's the uplift in poverty? It's Marx

* Cohen, D., Feldstein, L. and Putnam, R., *Better Together.* New York: Simon and Shuster, 2003

all over again – religion, the opiate of the masses; surely you don't buy into that?

Unlike you, Tzip, I think we Jews are finished if the Haredim continue to procreate at such a rapid rate... Jews are finished, Israel is finished – and Judaism is finished. There'll be a Black-People cult for a few generations, till they all starve or beat each other up/spit on each other (as is happening in Beit Shemesh and Mea She'arim already)... not sure what God'll do about that – He wasn't too proactive during the Holocaust, after all. Not sure how much God was involved in creating the rebirth of Israel – in fact, don't the Haredim agree with me here? The founders of modern Israel mostly didn't believe all that much in Him – they believed in the nation, and the people, and getting on with being wonderful, and taking the Jewish fate into Jewish hands. No matter how many times you say it, Tzip, I will not denigrate medical accomplishments, or culture, or start-up companies and fashion sense. Good for us, who accomplished all this, good good good for God who smiled as we did it, in spite of the difficulties He keeps flinging in our paths.

I invite goodness into my life, and being kind to people, and making the world a better place. Wearing cultish clothes, obsessing over covering my hair (I actually don't think I'm so sexy that my hair makes men forget how to think), fanaticizing about sex and elbows, turning touching into the biggest, hugest story in town – that's a raison d'être that I think has nothing whatsoever to do with God; it's a sham, it's a plot, it's a moral failure born of fear. Every story of Adam and Yaakov can be interpreted in a million different ways – or at least 70 – Yaakov can be seen as a cruel, lying manipulator, who deceives his own father – and not really a hero whom we'd like to emulate. Not me, at any rate.

And Hanukka can be seen as a total disaster, that almost totally destroyed us (mostly due to religious nutters.)

This last year has been pivotal for revealing how the religious have hijacked Judaism, and vulgarized and 'violentized' it; working on this book has scandalized me.

But I have hope in the marvelous, innovative, Jewish, spiritual, caring, traditional, spunky, funky, secular Am Yisrael; I believe we'll prevail and get the country back on track. Then we can drift back into shuls and pick up the texts, and enjoy them with love – not with viscious, rejectionist, holier-than-thou hysteria that has *nothing*, nothing to do with God, or religion, or Judaism itself.

Things are cyclical – and I think here in Israel the cycle is starting to change. We are living in that Chinese curse of 'interesting times,' we'll see what pans out.

Hurry on, Mashiach. Maybe he'll arrive in a bikini…

Love and hugs, always,

Pam

From: Danit Shemesh (danit.sh@spidimail.co.il)
To: Tzippi Sha-ked (tzippi@connectisra.co.il)

Tzippi, again, I'm speechless and my jaw is to the ground. The chutzpa! Pam, there are, of course, seventy ways of looking at the stories in the Torah. So, the way one views a story about Yaacov Avinu (our forefather Jacob) is more indicative of the beholder than of Yaacov. The Torah shares these stories for a specific reason: to teach. The teaching begins in the second book, *Shemot*, which provides guidelines for living. The examples of our forefathers and mothers teach us what to eschew and what to embrace. They paved our path through their mistakes and their hardships. All imaginable human frailties are revealed so we can learn from them. It's a simulation manual for our own lives. Torah is an experiential process as much as a cerebral one. Yaacov struggled with truth and integrity as this was what G-d intended. Yaakov teaches us how to deal with lies and false representations of reality. It was not a character flaw but rather what he crashed up against time and again. His challenges reveal to us how to be real in the face of falsehood. Your perversion of his good name by calling him a manipulator or a liar is indicative of the superficial way in which you studied the text. Of course I can expect that attitude from people whose heroes don't teach them how to live but rather how to write, paint, lead a country or even to play football.

Pam, I invite you to study the book of Genesis, to get a rudimentary understanding of Yaacov before you hurl verbal dirty diapers at his good name. You may also want to look into the reason behind the behaviors of the Haredim before you verbally spit at them because they make you uncomfortable. It may be that their ways are foreign to you, but the impetus of the behavior is rooted in a thought process that is unseen, hidden to the unscrutinizing eye. If the behavior is repugnant this is usually the manifestation of a thought process not wedded to halacha. Even if the behaviors seem foreign, it behooves us to understand them better, by decoding the cultural mores. If you don't care enough to question, don't spit, simply stay away. However, we are sisters, we're in this together whether we like it or not. The difference between family and friends is choice. Where we have no choice, we are more bound. 'Blood runs thicker than water' – which great mind said that? Probably one of your heroes, Pam.

Write to me!

Sincerely,

Danit

From: Tzippi Sha-ked (tzippi@connectisra.co.il)
To: Danit Shemesh (danit.sh@spidimail.co.il)
Pam Peled (pam-peled@bettaletter.com)
Subject: Too much

Hi Ladies,

Very, very down after hearing about the anti-Haredi demonstrations in Beit Shemesh and Haredim protests. Think that it's time to pack.... no future here on any account.... Tzip

From: Danit Shemesh (danit.sh@spidimail.co.il)
To: Tzippi Sha-ked (tzippi@connectisra.co.il)
Pam Peled (pam-peled@bettaletter.com)

Tzippi, what are you down about? The fact that Haredim are spitting on women/girls? I need to know what Pamela is talking about that is on the news and then I can respond.

I heard something about Tanya who was spat on by Haredim in Ashdod, and the spitting *meshuganas* in Beit Shemesh. I'm surprised they did not open booths selling Tanya T-shirts and GO-GIRL: bumper stickers. She's the hero of the day...how did she find herself in Ashdod? It's absolutely the strictest, most closed off place in Israel. No one goes there unless they have family, and no-one has secular family there. That community wanted their own private bus line, and to manage it themselves. Egged said they would fulfill any demands, and there was no need for a private line. So they believed Egged, which then opened the fourth line in the country to separate men and women. Interesting that go-girl Tanya had a camera handy* just when the weak link bit the bait and spat, after most of the men sat and said nothing. And Voila! We have news, we have a hero and a villain and a plot. Eureka! Just when Israel was getting bored. When you look for a fire, you will find it.

To me people's *yetzer hara*, both Tanya's and the bearded masked man's, is not news.

Are we in a sand box or are we adults? I am not here to represent anybody. I am asking everybody to stop being cry-babies, or terrified, or wish to move away because something does not go your way. The *meshugana* spitting on little girls will get what he deserves, hopefully from his own people who do not condone such behavior. Obviously, it would be insanely simplistic to assume that all Haredim spit, or condone it.

Do I go around claiming that all your children are dangerous because there are metal detectors in some schools? This was one incident, isolated and yes, extremely unfortunate. There are no excuses, none. The specific dark side of one man is directly related to his surroundings. The community sets the stage for whatever types of darknesses that lurk. We all have darkness of one kind or another. If you look for darkness you will find it, but don't you have better things to do with your time?

Danit

From: Pam Peled (pam-peled@bettaletter.com)
To: Tzippi Sha-ked (tzippi@connectisra.co.il)
CC: Danit Shemesh (danit.sh@spidimail.co.il)

Tzippi, darling, – I'm surprised at you, and here's why: you are in a win-win situation. If you really believe in God you can never be down – 'cause you have to believe that this is all part of His plan, and He surely can't mess up, can He? If you don't believe it's part of a Divine overall certainty, then the religious fanatics will lose their power, and things will settle down again in our lovely country… I'm sure of it.

* This was written before everyone had a camera in their phone.

It's funny – I'm so not religious, and yet I have a deep love and connection for Israel and the Jewish people; I never think of packing and leaving when things seem hard. *Le'hefech*, that's when I feel it's so necessary to be here. I've always felt that I couldn't live with myself if Israel collapsed, and I was alive, and not here to play my part. It's unfathomable to me that religious Jews can pray for Israel 3 times a day, pray for rain in Israel, pray for peace in Israel – and live somewhere else... I have to believe they care more about money and security (and yes, even seeing women on billboards) than they would care to admit – much more than making the effort to actually live here. Harav Kook said that everyone who lives in Israel is a 'religious' Jew... and, by extrapolation, I would say you can't be really 'religious' if you don't live here!

Cheer up – worse things have happened to the Jews than a few thousand mad Haredim. We're onto them; they'll have to see the light soon. It's the major story of the moment, on the news all the time, in editorials – have you been following? Are you still not reading the news, Danit?

I still believe that Israel is the greatest miracle of the millennium, and I still believe that the Mashiach is actually here... embodied in our wonderful people who are thriving in our own land, despite all obstacles.

Let's meet! Name a few dates... we need to hug.

Cheering up!!! Go for a fast walk, and look at the beauty all around...

Pam xxxxx

From: Danit Shemesh (danit.sh@spidimail.co.il)
To: Tzippi Sha-ked (tzippi@connectisra.co.il)
CC: Pam Peled (pam-peled@bettaletter.com)

Hi, Ladies, I sat down this morning to finish my last chapter when I saw Tzippi's link to Yossi Sarid claiming women are treated like 'filthy little things' in halacha – http://www.haaretz.com/print-edition/opinion/orthodox-judaism-treats-women-like-filthy-little-things-1.404505.* This *filthy* article truly made me want to suck up all the water in the kineret and cleanse myself. A flood would not be enough to undo the evil of this article.

How many times does humanity need to start over before we get it

---

* See Appendix 1.

right? G-d created the world with words, thereby teaching us their tremendous power. He gave us freedom of choice to use His tools to create or to destroy. The reason we are called *medaber* as opposed to *hai* or *tzome'ach* is that our essence lies in our speech. Your elected representative, dear secular society, the one to whom you gave a stage and a microphone, is destroying our world.

Before I speak of content, I want to respond to the process. Sarid's words serve only to confuse, separate, and distort. There's no redeeming value to his approach. He may sound informative, but actually he's misleading, and his ulterior motive is obvious. This diatribe serves only to throw an axe into the soft underbelly of Israeli society and to rip out an essential organ. It has little to do with Truth and a lot to do with politics; it's meant to poison the reader's mind against his brethren.

Are we suffering from lupus, where the body rejects its own organs? This is Haredi bashing, full stop. It's ugly and could lead to war. It's the quintessential example of 'a little information is a dangerous thing.' It takes things out of context and twists them into an unrecognizable state. *HaRav HaGaon Shlita* Rav Yossi Sarid denigrated what has been held sacred by Jews throughout history.

Yossi Sarid took bits of *Pirkei Avot* and *Gemara*, truncated them to fit his sordid reasoning, haphazardly stuck them back together, breathed his detestation into them and created a woman-clobbering Frankenstein. It is very difficult to relate to the content because it doesn't lend itself to reasoning or explanation. It's a declaration which leaves no room for discussion or communication.

This Haredi cannot in good conscience read unabashed untruths without standing up for what she believes.

Yossi and other secular Jews cannot possibly see from their side of the prism how we view women. Even the translation was incorrect. I tried five times to rebut some of his accusations but everything I say sounds like creative licensing and sugarcoating. I will not be made victim by being misconstrued.

Another *pirkei avot* warns against sitting in the presence of clowns, which is what this guy is. Shlomo *Hamelech* said, 'this too shall pass.' The Truth will remain.

– Danit

From: Pam Peled (pam-peled@bettaletter.com)
To: Danit Shemesh (danit.sh@spidimail.co.il)
Tzippi Sha-ked (tzippi@connectisra.co.il)

Look, Yossi Sarid makes it clear that this is the extreme position of the *Sikarikim* (or whatever the hell those maniacs are called.) He acknowledges that the Torah has 70 faces and various interpretations... but it's bloody hard to interpret anything good about the way those extreme Haredim seem to treat their women. All very fabulous to say "*Eshet Chayil*" on Fri night after the wife is almost collapsing from getting everything ready by the witching hour... Sarid isn't wrong about lots of the things he says. I know the arguments – that it's in women's favor that men thank God for not making them a woman, but, let's face it, these feminist interpretations are probably a lot to do with wishful thinking.

To the onlooker it seems as if these berserk Haredim (the ones who spit, and want separate seating, and can't hear a woman sing) are just abusive lunatics – I pity their poor wives and daughters. We know it's not *all* Haredim... but we're not hearing too much condemnation from any of them.

But back to the sexuality issue: You know what – I slept with Martin, plenty, before we got married, or even engaged. And what did premarital sex get me? Any less respect from my future husband? – Definitely not! Any anxieties, any regrets, any anything bad, at all? Any loss of self-respect? Any hangups? – *no*, no and no. All it gave me was a lot of fun times... and a close relationship, and a good, happy, uncomplicated, unfraught, un-analyzed-endlessly marriage in the end. I heartily recommend it.

I'm a Meretz voter, and I always voted for Yossi Sarid. I would have voted more middle-of-the-road now, but these extreme fanatics have pushed me to vote Meretz yet again.

So that's my midnight thoughts. I'm so tired that I probably should edit this fiercely before I hit the 'send' button but, what the hell – we're all friends still, right?

Pam xxxxx

Danit adds:

The Torah was given in two forms: oral and written. Chazal wrote down the oral Torah in the *Gemara* – a collection of discussions on the written word. How does the *Gemara* (the oral word) view women? On the connection between men and women, in *Ketubot* (one of the *masechtot*), it is written: 'a man without a woman is a man without joy, a man without blessing, a man without good.'

Joy is connection, true togetherness. A woman's ability to connect comes from emotional intelligence. Once the man feels connected he wants more, and augments the connection.

The word *bracha,* blessing, comes from *ribui*, more. Joy entails an expansion of man to receive more good. Feeling 'good' gives purpose, belonging, mutual respect; in short, love. These gifts come through the woman only.

The book of *Shemot* states, 'in the merit of righteous women the nation of Israel was redeemed and will be redeemed in the future.' When the Hebrews were enslaved and exhausted, the men wanted to divorce their wives and do only the work Pharoh stipulated, ignoring their real obligation, their families. They wrongly viewed work as their raison d'être.

The women, who never lost sight of love, went out to the fields under Miriam's tutelage and beckoned their men back to couple-hood, to connection, to family, where the only true joy lies. The men's eyes were opened to their folly and they came home to reconnect with their wives. Then G-d activated the Exodus. G-d will again activate redemption when *achva* and *ahava* begin in the home and flow over to the community.

The *Gemara* says women have tremendous, hidden power to implement *achva* and *ahava*. The words said under the *chuppa* extol this bonding, this potential for joy: *gila* (pleasure), *rina* (song), *ditza* (dance), *chedva* (sharing), *ahava* (love), *achva* (brotherhood), *shalom* (peace), and *reut* (unity).

If a Haredi man learns this before marriage, would he belittle his wife even for an instant? He realizes she's a divine gift and he cherishes her and takes care not to shatter the crystal. If he does shatter it that is because of his own evil inclination, or hers, but that is a different chapter.

I'm here to talk about the text of Judaism, not about human nature, or how well the message is received.

Chapter Ten

Very Caffeinated Questions for the Three Maidels

"... what saw you to tell us?
What stays with you latest and deepest? Of curious panics
Of hard-fought engagements or sieges
tremendous what deepest remains?"

Walt Whitman, *The Wound Dresser*

Pam writes:

An aside: in today's "Jerusalem Post," (26/11/2011), David Breakstone writes "the proliferation of religious extremism in our country today poses a real and present danger that, if not contained, will become the weapon of our mass destruction.

If Israel is to survive – if there is to be any reason for its survival – it needs to remain a Jewish state. And if the perception of what being Jewish means is going to be determined by an increasingly reactionary and narrow-minded fiefdom of politically motivated and power-hungry functionaries who are promoting a fundamentalist and corrupted notion of Judaism, then the vast majority of our next generation is going to want nothing to do with it. Increasingly mobile in an increasingly global age, they are going to drive that message home by leaving home, opening the door to myriad opportunities knocking in far-flung corners of the world. Places where God – or more accurately, her self-appointed envoys – has learned not to interfere with the way people live their lives."

David Breakstone is vice chairman of the World Zionist Organization, and a member of The Jewish Agency Executive. When I expressed such sentiments Tzippi's Orthodox friend declared she needed to shower after reading such 'filth' which caused her so much anguish that she could hardly read without retching. Is Breakstone also a 'rabid anti-Semite,' as I was branded?

So, to our answers:

1. Define: Who is a Jew? Please state your source and criteria.

DANIT: A Jew is one born to a Jewish mother... period. It's not a choice. It's a state of being. There are no degrees. Either you are Jewish or you are not. There is nothing in between. Jewishness is a gift of belonging, of specialness, of clarity.

PAM: C'mon, Tzip – you know this question is so loaded that it's not even fair. We all know the Orthodox answer – a Jew is halachically Jewish if his/her mother was halachically Jewish. That means Orthodox. So that's the answer. I have a friend from South Africa whose parents were born into the Orthodox community, of Orthodox parents. They later joined the Reform congregation (much like the Conservative *shul* in the States.) My friend grew up so Jewish that she came on Aliya; one of her siblings '*hazar betshuva*' and is a black-suited rabbi in California today. Her daughter is marrying a nice Israeli boy, but the rabbis here have cast aspersions on her Jewishness, as the mother grew up "Reform." This young woman, who is as "Jewish" as they come – done the army, speaks Hebrew, did a *bagrut* in *Tanach* – might not be able to go under the *Chuppa* in Israel.

So here's my answer: I define a Jew as someone who has a halachic connection with Judaism and wants to belong to the Jewish people. If the connection isn't 100% kosher, like Russian *olim* with a paternal Jewish grandfather, run crash courses, dunk them in the *mikve*, and make them ours. (I prefer that any day over stuffed envelopes of greenbacks paid to chief rabbis, as happened in my own family.) We need more Jews – let's welcome them with open arms.

TZIPPI: This isn't easy for me. Halacha clearly states that a Jew is born of a Jewish mother. Yet I concur with Rabbi Chaim Amsalem who suggests recognizing people born of a Jewish father as harboring the seed of Abraham, and facilitating their conversion in a manner not fraught with halachic red tape. Still, at this juncture, the Torah has defined for us who is a Jew.

2. Who is a Rabbi? Are Rabbis across the entire religious spectrum equally deserving of the title?

DANIT: A Rabbi learns all the necessary texts and passes exams. He then receives *smicha*, his diploma. The texts have been the same throughout history and include the laws of *kashrut*, *niddah*, Shabbat, *shchita*, *dinim* (money), and more. This presumes that the Rabbi learns God's law, which is not written by man. It is not negotiable. It is only accessible.

A Rabbi is also a teacher, or mentor. He is not a revolutionary, a psychologist, or a politician. His title presumes leadership qualities, humility, and a deep desire to give of himself. He does not merely know the text, but also how to apply it with dignity and respect to humankind.

Any deviation from the original texts does not produce what we call a Rabbi.

"*Ase lecha rav...*" from the Ethics of the Fathers asks you to build an infrastructure in life with a two-pronged effect; being proactive and creating a system of checks and balances. '*Ase*' means to do; it presumes awareness. When a person is active in life's decisions, he/she is involved in designing their reality. The 'rav' (Rabbi) aspect of the passage adds an objective, cerebral viewpoint, keeping one honest, involved and sensitive.

This, of course, assumes that you can't simply pick a rav from the pile. The word '*lecha*' (for yourself) means this directive needs to be custom-tailored for you. The rav must understand your inner workings, your orientation on the map of life before you can feel comfortable sharing your decision-making process.

I once heard an analogy of '*Ase lecha rav*': You're a blind mouse in a maze struggling to find the exit. You feel less agitated because there is someone who has been through the maze and knows the way. That someone knows your situation, cares, and can help guide you by explaining the pitfalls and turns ahead. That someone is wise, compassionate, and one step ahead. Your confidence in that someone makes you feel safer in the maze. That someone you should make your personal Rav.

Naturally, there are also women who lead others towards their goals in life. There are all sorts of leaders in a community; however, they aren't called 'Rav'. A Rav can and must also give a *psak halacha,* which refers back to his supreme knowledge of Torah.

PAM: A few years ago I was invited to lecture on "Shakespeare and the Jews" at Limmud in an aging hotel in the Catskills. This lovely experience left me with a new friend – a Barbara Streisand look-alike powerhouse – who started studying to be a rabbi at fifty. Today she marries couples, does baby-namings and Bar Mitzvas, and walks converts through their paces as they study the tenets of Judaism. She is writing a book, this funky Jewish granny, entitled "Funny, You Don't Look Like a Rabbi." She doesn't.

A few years ago I would have dismissed her claims to the pulpit with disdain and derision. But here's the thing: she *loves* Judaism. She breathes it. She studies *Mishna,* and *Gemara,* and the *parashat hashavua* every week. She adores Israel; she endlessly leads missions here. She doesn't really keep 100% kosher, and she certainly doesn't keep Shabbat, but she feels as though she is doing her part to spread the word and make others aware of their *Yiddishkeit.* Her congregants would not be more Jewish if their rabbi was Orthodox; they wouldn't set foot in an Orthodox establishment. They are from "mixed" marriages, mostly; the Orthodox would prefer them to leave Judaism altogether – offspring of a 'Gentile' mom and Jewish dad are not welcome in Orthodox shuls.

So, my dogmatic rejection of women Rabbis, Reform and Liberal Rabbis, along with Reform and Liberal Judaism itself, has softened. Where I once scorned other streams of Judaism, I don't anymore. It's still not really for me; call me old-fashioned or just plain two-faced, but I prefer my Rabbis male. I can't rationalize why I prefer my Torah portion of the week read out by men, but I do. (Which leads to the obvious question: why isn't it sexy to hear a man sing from the *Bimah* of a *shul,* about, for example, sex in the Garden of Eden, or kings screwing concubines? Why isn't there the equivalent of *Kol Ha'isha* for men?) So, apart from deep and sexy cadences, I suppose the reason I prefer men's voices leading my prayers boils down to habit. I still prefer South African Cadbury's chocolate after a lifetime in the land of Elite.

I look at Rabbis in Israel – good, bad and indifferent – Orthodox rabbis who are understanding and reach out, and those who say that car crashes and bombs and the helicopter disaster happened because of desecrating Shabbat – and *Hiddush* Rabbis and Rabbis for peace... and I say that it doesn't matter to me from which strata of the spectrum they come – let them be deserving of honour, let them love the Torah, and let them be *menschen.* Then I will embrace them.

TZIPPI: If 'Rabbi' is defined as 'teacher' I have no problem with that appellation for all. If 'Rabbi' connotes a spiritual authority on halachic opinion, only an orthodox Rabbi fulfills this criterion. I don't give a blank check to every orthodox Rabbi as I don't believe that being orthodox alone provides him with a mandate to administer spiritually to others. Without personal integrity, compassion and wisdom no Orthodox Rabbi, in my opinion, has the Bible on his side.

3. Should Torah and Jewish values play a central role in how the country is governed?

DANIT: Israel is a Jewish State and proud to be so. We are different from other countries, and should embrace this, rather than be ashamed. The English system of government has been around for a long time, but our system – one that is divine – has endured much longer. Why should we live under a bastardized system, a clumsy collection of bits and pieces of jurisprudence from Europe and America, rather than be true to our unique set of values? We are the gem of the Middle East. We should not imitate other countries which have not proven themselves in terms of civil rights (internal affairs), or in the use of power (foreign affairs.)

PAM: No. Not a central role. The separation of church and state in a democracy is a basic tenet that needs to be introduced into the Holy Land pronto de pronto. A coda is necessary: these highly caffeinated questions deserve more than a facile paragraph or two. But, working within these constraints, here is my take on this '*plonta.*'

Of course Israel should be informed by Jewish culture, values, and tradition. Of course our day of rest will always be Shabbat, the *chagim* will determine our calendars, our code of ethics will influence our work ethics and our lives. Of course we should teach our children *Torah* and how to pray; the daily prayers shouldn't just belong to a certain segment of society. But this should be done out of love and respect and tolerance, not by religious coercion which only serves to push people – to thrust people – away from all religion, although sometimes it throws them into the arms of Buddhism, or meditation, or other spiritual sanctuaries. Every beautiful mystic and spiritual thread can be found in Judaism, but not legislated into people's heads.

TZIPPI: Yes, in the same way that the Founding Fathers of America valued the Bible and created an infrastructure that was inspired, not impeded, by religious values. I advocate separation between church and state in our Holy Land. Judaism should be the blueprint that inspires and permeates the way we govern this country. I want Jews across the divide to embrace Judaism, but never through state coercion. However, I would like the Sabbath and Kashrut to be respected by state institutions.

4. Is Torah: A) Divinely inspired B) The Gospel Truth C) A collection of quaint myths D) A guideline for picking and choosing what we are comfortable believing and practicing?

DANIT: Torah is A) divinely inspired and B) the gospel truth.

PAM: None of the above. I don't know what the Torah really is; but for sure it's partly a collection of stories, and ancient history. I know the Torah has parallels in other sources: Mesopotamian, for example. Perhaps there is a Divine element involved; I'm much too insignificant to know. It's too big for me – I don't spend much time thinking about it.

TZIPPI: I think it's A. I shudder at Jews who think they alone know G-d's will, and can't make room for others. Similarly, I balk at the convictions of secular Jews who claim there is no G-d. They're both equally condescending.

5. How do you view the following streams of Judaism: Reform, Conservative, Modern Orthodox, Haredi, Reconstructionist, and Messianic (Jews for Jesus)?

DANIT: Reform Judaism is apologetic. It lives a double existence and is an attempt to appease guilt about straying from the tried and true. The Reform Jew feels a pull to the great big world, but is not ready to relinquish his Jewish identity. The result is a confused Jew living life as a gentile, suffering from extreme identity issues, and calling those who are sure of their identity (Haredim) 'primitive.'

Conservative Jews want to stay loyal to the confines of Judaism. However, they cannot ignore current times. There's a discrepancy between 'going with the flow' of life, and Jewish laws. Jewish law becomes 613 issues that need to be mainstreamed into real life, 613 problems to be solved. This creates frustration, and a dual existence.

Modern Orthodox Jews value the land of Israel more than anything. I respect and even admire their directedness. But they've lost sight of the most important priority, Torah. I believe they put so much faith and effort into the State that they don't see that G-d will decide when Israel is wholly ours. To make this state viable they need the partnership of the larger society, which comes with a big price. I believe they care too much what the secular community thinks of them, and try too hard to appease them. If appeasement is a policy, it leads to the dilution of one's mores (*ani maamin.*)

I view Messianic Jews with disgust. They betray their origins and covet the 'strong.' This 'religious Darwinism' is antithetical to everything I hold dear. It comes from ignorance and self-loathing.

I view Haredi Judaism with quiet respect. I cannot completely agree with everything, but it's the best system I know for enabling my faith to flourish, and helping my children become well-adjusted individuals. It is unapologetic and direct. Expectations of the individual are clear and obligatory. Of course, this comes with a price but one I am willing to pay for singularity of mind, and clarity.

PAM: I answered this in Question 2. The more I see how Orthodoxy in Israel is deteriorating into Cult, how women are being excised from life, how too many rabbis are corrupt and sometimes plain bad, how the Ultra Orthodox live largely in poverty and deprivation, the more anti-'Orthodox' I become, and the more embracing of gentler forms of Judaism. Reconstructionist and Jews for Jesus don't really count, do they? Their avowed premise is to turn Jews into Christians.

My solution? Maybe John Lennon was right when he warbled about a world with "no religion too." Wouldn't that be lovely? Just let's keep the traditions, and the food.

TZIPPI: Well, here's the thing: I appreciate many people in the Reform, Conservative, and Reconstructionist movements. I even admire some of their philosophies and activism. I would like it a whole lot better if they called their religion something other than (normative) Judaism. I was once involved in a research project which showed that a disproportionate number of board members of Conservative Synagogues were non-halachic converts. This suggests that many members of the board, and even of the congregation, may not be halachically Jewish. Still, I hesitate to classify their movements as non-Jewish. However, I draw the line at the atheistic Reconstructionists and the Jews for Jesus – they definitely do not practice any form of Judaism.

6. T/F: The Torah was dictated by G-d, physically written by Moses.

DANIT: True, of course.

PAM: I find these questions so funny: in 20 words state your opinion on God. (Wasn't this Question 4?) I don't know if there is a God – I should know if He wrote the Torah?

TZIPPI: True.

7. What Jewish practices should a Jew keep in order to be considered a practicing Jew?

DANIT: It is said the 'identity card' of a practicing Jew is to be '*shomer Shabbat*' which means that he/she realizes that they are in the passenger seat. Although they work hard during the week, they just work here; they are not the Boss. On Shabbat they create nothing, initiate nothing, and move nothing. They are in stop-the-world-I'm-getting-off mode, and yet the world continues to turn. Once a week, we allow G-d to show us that He's in charge and what a beautiful performance it is – full of family, rest, good food, and true distraction-free connection.

The *shomer Shabbat* believes in the physical as well as the metaphysical. This world is not 'what you see is what you get,' but rather a beacon of light in the darkness.

PAM: Oooowwah. I know you would answer "Shabbat and Kashrut." I would have said 'a little bit of this, a little bit of that' before I lived in Israel. Today I say that 'practicing Jews' are messing up the country... they practice and practice but don't get it right. Would fighting in the IDF qualify? Or living here and growing up with Jewish traditions; does that cut it? But it's complicated: are foreign workers' kids, growing up with Jewish traditions, "Jewish?" Of course not. So halacha would have to come into it. How? Too hard for me.

TZIPPI: A Jew practices his/her Judaism when engaged in mitzvot. How many or how few is between him and his maker.

8. Should a Jew be limited to only Jewish practices and ideas?

DANIT: The word 'limit' is inaccurate because there's no limit to practice and ideas in Judaism. However, of course, one could wander the earth and never fully discover Truth, only hints of it. So why not begin with what you already are, Jewish, and then see if you need anything else?

PAM: What?! Don't understand the question.

TZIPPI: Not at all. *Torah umadah* –Torah and secular knowledge. We are placed into this world with a mandate to fix what is broken, elevate the profane. We can only do that if we are steeped in the sciences and other wisdoms. Some of the greatest Jewish rabbis were educated in medicine, science, and philosophy. The *chup* is to learn the difference between education and capitulation. Secular wisdom must serve you as a Jew, not vice versa.

9. What is your idea of authentic Judaism?

DANIT: Living and breathing the Torah, (the Teacher,) which is a manual to guide us. In *Vayikra* (Leviticus) it is written: *'va chai bahem'* – 'and you should live by them.' *Chai* means life. A person's life force is ultimately rooted in mitzvot (commandments.) A person's power and sense of purpose lie in the mitzvot, which connect thought, action and feeling.

PAM: Oy, not again. Answered this already, twice.

TZIPPI: It is a belief that the Torah was given to us by G-d and serves as a daily barometer for our life choices. Sporting a beard and hat and acting contrary to Jewish tenets does not make an authentic Jew. Judaism also does not exclude women in jeans and t-shirts who keep other mitzvot.

For me it is not about externals, but about the interior life which informs one's actions. I have a huge problem when Jews see other Jews suffering and, instead of helping with resources and time, state that they "are davening" in support. Worse is that some Jews don't consider others Jewish, and can thus side-step the obligation to be your brother's keeper (not *Kippa*!)

10. I do/do not keep all/most/some/few/none of the Halachot.

DANIT: I do keep some of the halachot. I want to keep as many as possible; however, there are halachot for men and for *Kohanim* and *Leviim* which do not pertain to me. I hold dear, and with all my might try to keep those that do.

PAM: As Romeo said to Juliet, "For what purpose, love?" Why do you ask me this – what do you care? Whose business is it what halachot I keep? This smacks of competitive kashrut to me. How much does 'giving to charity' count, is that keeping halachot? And visiting the sick? Does that counterbalance 'not putting on lights of Shabbat?' If I honored my mother and father, and don't covet my neighbor's ass, nor murder or commit adultery, is that keeping 'few' of the halachot; or 'some' of them? And if I light candles on Shabbat, but after the sun has set – where does that fit in?

Can't answer this question.

TZIPPI: I do keep some.

11. I do not keep most/some/any of the Halachot because: A) I don't find the mitzvot compelling B) Don't believe they are from G-d C) Too lazy to keep them D) Find them too restrictive E) Don't understand them F) I prefer to pick and choose the ones I am comfortable with G) Not yet ready to embrace them.

DANIT: I do not keep some of the *halachot* simply because I may not know them. 'Not yet ready to embrace' does not apply to *halachot* but to social mores. The community expects certain stringencies, not necessarily in the Torah, which are difficult for me.

PAM: Mmm... more of question 10. I suppose I don't believe they're from God. Is not wearing trousers a God-given halacha? I don't believe it. Is having 2 dishwashers a God-given halacha? I don't believe that either. Is leaving the table, as poor ole' Gila Manolson's 'sensitive' rabbi husband does, on Shabbat, so his female guests can really go wild and sing *zmirot* without turning him on sexually (God Forbid)... is that keeping a halacha? We don't subscribe to that one. In my house women are allowed to sing in Martin's company, but it's more likely to be a Beatles' oldie on the radio than a *zmira*.

TZIPPI: I suppose the answers are C, D, E and G, though I'm sure that some mitzvot are not divinely inspired. This opens up a whole can of halachic worms, I know.

12. Views about Judaism: A) It's a winner and we need to stick with it. B) It is an evolving tradition and we should change whatever is antiquated to fit in with the times. C) I believe in being open-minded, therefore all sectors/denominations are equally valid expressions of Judaism. D) Simply does not have a monopoly on truth.

DANIT: It is Truth; therefore we need to stick with it. By definition, there is only One Truth. I have no problem with being open-minded, but not at the expense of the mind. Do you know the expression, 'you're so open-minded your brains are falling out?'

PAM: A – certainly. But what is 'Judaism?' See, to me it's not leaving the table when a woman opens her mouth to sing in praise of the Lord.

What if she's an ugly woman? Or an old, old granny? Would a sensitive husband still have to excuse himself; do *all* women turn religious men on, uncontrollably? Shame! I think the religious are prostituting women fair and square... but that's another issue. Judaism was never the 'law of the land' – Jews had to abide by the civilian laws of wherever they lived; Judaism was the spice, the essence, the extra. The only time that halacha was in control was before Jews were kicked out of ancient Israel; we were defeated because of '*sinat chinam,*' when religious zealots went mad. Pity we haven't learned our lesson.

TZIPPI: The answers for me are A and a qualified B. Yes, times are evolving and certain dispensations must be accorded, but in the spirit of halacha. I believe Judaism must be lived in a way that isn't stifling, but we can't exactly improvise as we go along, can we?

13. Do you believe that Jews should live on a higher plane of spirituality from the rest of the world? Yes/No

DANIT: We have the Torah, so more is expected of us. We have the tools to be more spiritual; the burden is on us to do so. The answer is a resounding YES.

PAM: I'd like everyone to live on a higher plane of spirituality. Jews? Sure, that would be great. What do I see in Israel? Religious Jews are so often bogged down in their ready-steady-go: "It's Shabbat!" and checking if it's exactly 6 hours to the dot since they ate meat that they have no time for being '*bnei adam*' – I see religious drivers racing like maniacs, and religious businessmen screwing others, and religious fanatics visiting prostitutes. I know, the secular do all of the above too. Conclusion: *Religion doesn't make people more moral – it only makes them wait longer between eating meat and milk.*

TZIPPI: YES. I think that we should live to our best potential. So should every other society too.

14. Are the tenets of Zionism compatible with Judaism? Yes/No

DANIT: Zionism without Torah is problematic. Why should we have the land? Because G-d said so. No other reason could appease those who lived here before us. The timing of Zionism is not up to us; it is written in the Torah and has not yet been revealed.

PAM: Whose Judaism? Mine – certainly. Danit's – of course not. She's happy for Israel to disappear, until the Messiah arrives. Meanwhile she will wait in Arab controlled land. Luckily for her she doesn't read papers or watch the news – she doesn't know that Abbas declared that when he's in charge, the territories will be "Judenfrei." My kids did the army; Martin and I pay our taxes. Do yeshiva *bochers* pay income tax? Most sure as hell don't go to the army.

TZIPPI: Yes, of course yes.

15. The greatest problem facing the Jewish nation today is: A) Islamic Terrorism B) Threat of nuclear extinction C) Internal social/economic unrest D) The Haredi/secular divide E) Political infighting/stagnation.

DANIT: Our greatest problem is brotherly strife and misbehavior. That is the main reason the Temple Mount was destroyed, and is the main reason it has not yet been rebuilt.

PAM: None of the above. The greatest threat facing Israel today is the Haredism of the country. I'm not alone in this view. Ephraim Halevy said the same, and he knows a thing or two about threats. He is the ex-head of the Mossad.

TZIPPI: All of the above. I think that we are in the midst of a *balagan* of epic proportion. G-d help us.

16. My deepest desire for our Jewish state is: A) Acceptance by the rest of the nations of the world B) To be recognized as a technological/social/ economic/medical wonder in the world C) To have our fellow Jews live up to their Jewish potential.

DANIT: To have our fellow Jews live up to their Jewish potential, to be a light unto other nations. To create a dwelling for G-d down here with us.

PAM: None of the above, and all of the above. My deepest desire is that our Jewish state is a peaceful, happy, thriving, miraculous, modern and traditional all-at-once democracy, where everyone can reach their potential (women and men, Muslims, Christians, atheists and Jews), and where the majority of people are proud Jews, not narrow-minded cultist bigots in long black coats.

TZIPPI: I want it all. Why not!

17. What is your visceral reaction when you see a scantily-clad Israeli walking in public places? A) Sorry that they don't have proper decorum B) Horrified C) Indifferent D) Embarrassed E) Wish you had the body to go with the outfit F) Remorse that they don't live up to the Torah definition of modest attire.

DANIT: When I see a scantily-clad Israeli I feel pained that we live like the *goyim*, that we have not yet differentiated ourselves and are still imitating them in dress and behavior.

PAM: Oh my goodness! I don't think about it. If it's hot I dress scantily too; is a beach a public place? Is a bathing-costume 'scanty?' Whoa...who the hell cares what people wear?

TZIPPI: I feel saddened that they aren't more respectful of their bodies. You don't have to dress like a Haredi to not be an exhibitionist. I have a problem with billboards of the scantily-clad paraded in front of my boys. I'm fine with women on billboards, just in some semblance of attire, please.

18. When you see a tired Haredi woman with a potato sack over her hair, a nondescript outfit choking her collar bone and seven (plus) children in tow, you feel: A) Horrified B) Indifferent C) Angry D) Embarrassed for her E) Pity F) Sympathetic G) Jealous H) Thank G-d you don't look like that and wonder if she knows she is unattractive. I) Proud that she is living a Torah lifestyle.

DANIT: This question is misleading, so I beg to rephrase. When I see a Haredi woman looking tired and dragging seven plus children behind her, I feel empathic; I know how she feels. I wonder if she is caring enough for herself, if she has the right guidance or is winging it alone. I also know that if she survives this part, great satisfaction and reward await her. It is not for nothing. She will always be surrounded by loving children and grandchildren. She will not die alone and will not feel the empty nest syndrome. She will be appreciated for the rest of her life, and remembered for generations.

PAM: None of the above. She can dress however she likes. But I resent hugely how her life-style is impinging on the democratic, social, and economic wellbeing of my country.

TZIPPI: My answer is mixed. I'm horrified that she may not have time or inclination to take care of herself, and I'm proud she's living a Torah lifestyle. Looking feminine and less haggard is compatible with Torah ideals. I'm sorry she's not a better ambassador to the secular world.

19. What is your ideal Israeli family: values, Judaism, children, and goals?

DANIT: That family is proud to be Jewish and Israeli. It lives according to ideals set out on a red carpet from the beginning of time. A family is a collection of individuals who all hold dear the same set of values. The perfect family is unthreatened by the contradictions of individuals due to a foundational Torah which all members respect and adhere to, each in their own individual way.

PAM: Oh; the perfect family. Goodness. Is there such a thing? Healthy mommy, healthy daddy, healthy kids. Healthy grandparents on both sides, and healthy uncles and aunts with their own healthy kids. And everyone 'normative' – no abuse, no substance abuse, no craziness. Good communication all round – love and caring and good wishes for the welfare of all. Lots of family time – around the dinner table every night, around the Shabbat table, on the beach, on *chagim*, in the pool. Family holidays. Family events – birthdays, celebrations, promotions, degrees. Traditions – Jewish traditions, family traditions, personal traditions. Lots of laughter. Fun, and hard work, and being there for each other in good times and bad. Happy, healthy children, polite and friendly and hard-working and good, closeness to parents, closeness to siblings, closeness to family. Well-rounded and well-adjusted. With good friends, and good partners when the time comes, and good families of their own. Everyone feeling fulfilled – good education, good jobs, good salaries. Everyone enjoying their lives. And health, health, health. Wouldn't that be nice.

TZIPPI: The ideal Israeli family is inclusive and tolerant of other members of the tribe. The family works hard, plays hard and prays hard, and lives to the highest standards of Jewish ideals. The family is also wedded to the *hashkafa* of creating a better society – *tikkun olam*. Respect, education, investment in health and one another's well being are a few of the attributes of this ideal family.

20. Why was I born into this world? A) It was a random event but now that I'm here I'll make the most of it B) I was sent here for a purpose, though I'm not sure what it is. C) To serve G-d in a manner that I deem fit. D) To serve G-d according to the Torah E) Other.

DANIT: I was born into this world for a specific purpose that only I can fulfill. If I do not fulfill it, the entire world leans slightly on its axis and suffers a lack of balance. I was given the tools and the desire to be wholly me. That was divinely ordained before I entered my mother's womb. The only path to *me* is via the service of G-d.

PAM: I don't know. I think I serve God every day by being a good person, and not being a drain on other Jews or anyone else. If by serving God the Haredim mean imposing on the rest of the Jewish people, then the Jewish people would be better off without God.

TZIPPI: I don't purport to have all the answers but I believe we are placed on earth to serve G-d. Each of us has a task that only we can fulfill. But no man is an island and we have to join forces to actualize our true potential. We need one another at the most intrinsic level. Jews have been given a Jewish mandate to fulfill. We should act in a manner that befits our own Jewish ideals, while inspiring the world at large. We should remain cognizant of this fact, while celebrating this unique role.

From: Danit Shemesh (danit.sh@spidimail.co.il)
To: Pam Peled (pam-peled@bettaletter.com)
Tzippi Sha-ked (tzippi@connectisra.co.il)

Shavua tov to you, wonderful ladies. Not sure what I have learned more in this project, what it means to be a Haredi in Israel or how to speak my mind concisely and with zest.

Sincerely,
Danit

From: Pam Peled (pam-peled@bettaletter.com)
To: Danit Shemesh (danit.sh@spidimail.co.il)
CC: Tzippi Sha-ked (tzippi@connectisra.co.il)

Hello ladies – how are you both? What a lovely event on Sunday – I know I disappoint you both with my intransigent views, but I for one find the conversation very stimulating and essential, despite the (so far) lack of progress towards greater mutual tolerance. We'll get there. Meanwhile we can all agree that Modern Orthodox wins hands down when it comes to cooking – Danit, I haven't seen you in action – but Tzippi, you put the secular me to shame completely...even your tuna salad is better than mine, somehow. It's that divine element.

So, my friends, it appears that life is too complicated for us mere mortals. I hope we all can join in the afterlife, much wiser and more tolerant and laid-back, for endless lattes and gooey cakes...who cares about being fat in the hereafter? Do men and women go to the same heaven??? Are people dressed there??? Or is everyone (gasp!) naked as in the Garden of Eden? Are there Talmudic musings on this, I wonder?

Love you lots, and shavua tov,
Pam xxx

From: Pam Peled (pam-peled@bettaletter.com)
To: Tzippi Sha-ked (tzippi@connectisra.co.il)
Danit Shemesh (danit.sh@spidimail.co.il)

Reading over Danit's ch 1 I finally got a handle on why the Haredi life-style so disturbs me: Danit sounds so pure, so naive, so totally immersed in the 'eschew bad and search for the good' in life... sounds amazing, but let's not think for a moment that that's the Haredi way. Most lifestyles purport the same; the best converts are the ones who accept this at face value, believe it, and live so purely. Danit would have been a naive, wonderful person in any walk of life – it's not being Haredi that 'purified' her. She could have been good and giving without the prohibition on showing her toes. The leaders of the cult are not so good and pure – my good friends who raised almost a million dollars for a soup kitchen in Jerusalem have just been diddled out of a whack of money by Haredim (including a rabbi.) *I know* not all Haredim are crooks. But my mantra remains: people are people are people; the Haredi world is just another cult with zero to do with piety.

Danit will say she's not 'suffering,'but Scientology cultists believe they don't suffer either; I can't see any difference. Same uniform, same uniform ideas, same fear of the outside, same blind adherence to leaders, same belief that 'not changing' is the essence.

I saw, re-reading Danit's ch. 1, that she was lonely in L.A., and tired of running from country to country without good friends who could lend her eggs. She was ripe for community and belonging and support. She fell right into the open arms of Haredism... it could have been the kibbutz, or the orange people, or a Dati Leumi *yishuv*. But she happened to meet welcoming Haredim, and the rest is history; that's what makes life life. I'm not knocking friends, or supportive frameworks; I would be dead without my family and my friends. I've always had a supportive framework, I now see why I've never 'got' the safety-net of stringent laws of community; I wasn't fragile.

Who knows – I'm pretty fragile now. I can see the seductive appeal of a community of like-minded, like-dressed, like-tired (being tired makes you question less, no?) women bringing bagels... very comforting.

Oy, oy, oy. So many issues.

Laila tov, dear ladies,

Pam x

From: Danit Shemesh (danit.sh@spidimail.co.il)
To: Pam Peled (pam-peled@bettaletter.com)

Pamela, Rabi Hanania said (*Masechet Avoda perek gimel*), 'greater is he who is directed and obeys than he who is not directed and does.' Those who wake up in the morning, 'feel the love,' and go volunteer in the nearest soup kitchen are good. But 'greater' are those who don't want to bother,yet know that they answer to a Higher power so go to soup kitchens or to visit the sick. Why are they greater? Because they bettered themselves.

Our job in this world is to move towards a higher 'me,' a 'me' that is modestly hidden from public view. You say, I could have been 'good' with the orange people. You say I was desperate and fell into the arms of the Haredim. Don't you underestimate my freedom of choice? Of course I could have ended up in the arms of anything, but I chose to be 'greater,' to be directed as opposed to going with my nature and simply 'feeling good.'You say people are people are people, isn't it time we do something about it?

From: Tzippi Sha-ked (tzippi@connectisra.co.il)
To: Danit Shemesh (danit.sh@spidimail.co.il)
Pam Peled (pam-peled@bettaletter.com)

So many issues ladies... forget the lattes. You make me want to head straight for the gin.

Appendix 1

Orthodox Judaism treats women like filthy little things

By Yossi Sarid | Dec. 30, 2011 | 2:48 AM

If you would like to know the source from which your brothers derive their brazen behavior, go over to the study hall and open a page of Talmud. It's true that the Torah has 70 faces, but the trend of these faces is clear: The source of the pollution is in halacha (Jewish law) itself. What is happening in Beit Shemesh and its satellites is not "contrary to halacha," it is mandated by halacha. And the rest will be told to the grandmothers, daughters and granddaughters.

Anyone ignoramus knows that the Torah's "ways are ways of pleasantness," that "the honor of a king's daughter is within," and that "proper behavior comes before the Torah," but it's worth knowing more. It's worth knowing that a woman is unfit to be a judge, and is also unfit to give testimony. She is unfit for any public position with authority. "Thou shalt appoint a king over thee" – a king and not a queen.

A daughter, commanded the sages, must not be taught Torah, because "the mind of woman is not suited to be taught, but [only] to words of nonsense." Women are light-minded and have little knowledge.

And if a man and a woman are drowning in a river, first they'll save the man, "who is obligated to perform more commandments," whereas a woman's "wisdom is only in the spindle." In fact, "words of Torah should be burned rather than being given to women."

A man must say three blessings every day during morning prayers: He thanks God "that He didn't make me a gentile, that He didn't make me a woman, that He didn't make me an ignoramus." And it's not proper to speak to a woman too much, since "all her conversation is nothing but words of adultery," and whoever talks to her too much "causes evil to himself and will end up inheriting hell." And let's not even talk about the fate of someone "who looks even at a woman's little finger."

The extremists who spit at women, who call themselves Sikarikim, learned their lesson 101 times and learned it well: A husband would do well not to let his wife go outside, into the street, and should restrict her outings "to once or twice a month, as necessary, since a woman has no beauty except by sitting in the corner of her house."

Because inside the house – very deep inside – her glorious honor awaits her: "Every woman washes her husband's face and feet and pours him a cup and prepares his bed and stands and serves her husband. And any woman who refrains from doing any of these tasks that she is obligated to perform – is forced to do them." Some recommend forcing her with a whip or by starvation "until she gives in."

And needless to say, she is at her husband's disposal whenever he is overcome by a desire "to satisfy his urges with her." And if she continues to rebel, he always has the right "to divorce her without her consent."

And there are many similar halachot, only a few of which we have collected here. Nor have we cited everything in the name of the ones who said them, for lack of space. The readers are invited to find the references on Shabbat – and to browse around – on their own; this is a good opportunity for study. We will direct your attention to Tractate Shabbat, which does a good job of summing up halacha's attitude toward women: "a sack full of excrement" with a bleeding hole.

Some people will seek to console themselves: It's true that this is the halacha both m'doraita (from the Torah) and m'drabanan (from the rabbis), but that is not what is taught nowadays. But it suffices to listen to the sermon the sage Rabbi Ovadia Yosef delivered five years ago, based on the well-known halachic work "Kitzur Shulchan Aruch": "A man must take care not to walk between two women or between two dogs or two pigs, and men should also not allow a woman or a dog or a pig to walk between them."

Treating women as impure and filthy begins with halacha and continues with actions. As long as the religious and ultra-Orthodox parties – Shas, United Torah Judaism, Habayit Hayehudi and National Union, none of which have any women in the Knesset – are not disqualified, their nakedness will continue to sing out and the nakedness of the land will be revealed.

Epilogue

So, after three years of cyberspace *kibitzing*, we three ladies met once again in the same Modi'in Mall for another (kosher) lunch. The food was good, the coffee strong, but the talk was tough. Pam wishes our book could close on a more optimistic note; I am not sure a happy ending was ever our goal.

If our intent was really to tweak hearts and minds, and see the others budge on any major beliefs, we certainly struck out. But that was not the goal, at least not mine. My efforts from the word go were to place our voices on an equal platform so we could address issues pertinent to Jewish women in Israel. We recognize that there are many other voices in our diverse and dynamic land; I hoped our project would reach out to them all and enable fruitful and constructive communication. As we churned out our chapters, my vision was to learn about each other and become enriched by this experience.

We discussed, at Café Greg, the recent demonstration of some three thousand Haredim who had gathered in Jerusalem to protest the new mandatory draft for all Jewish citizens of Israel. The event polarized the country; viewed either as positively momentous, or entirely ruinous and despicable. Pam, of course, was sickened by Haredi intransigence and what she terms abrogation of civic responsibility. Danit, of course, proudly proclaimed her awe at the unity and gumption of her community. Negative media coverage left her cold; she hadn't expected anything else. As for me, while I support the Haredi right to protest, I am hugely saddened by the *massive* setback it caused for religious-secular relations.

But, *kacha zeh,* as they say here, it is what it is; we discussed, and disagreed, and ordered lunch.

I'm going to miss our cyber chats. It was cathartic laying our cards out on the table, and it helped us to clarify our own positions while learning about different ones. It's bloody impossible to change one strong-minded woman's opinion; forget three! Yet I tried to engage us all in meaningful debate and communication, rather than simply scoring points. I'm not sure I succeeded entirely, and it was no picnic being caught in the middle, but I'm glad we each had a seat at the table. We may always contest the seating arrangements, the other's attire, and even the menu, but we're still breaking bread and the lattes are still flowing... Our percolating dialogue continues and that gives me hope that others can take up the conversation where we left off.

Lechaim!

Tzippi

Glossary

Achva and Ahava – brotherhood and love
Al Haboker – first thing in the morning
Aliya – immigration to Israel
Allevaai Aleinu – please let it happen to us!
Ani maamin – my belief
Aseh lecha Rav – make for yourself a Rabbi
Avraham Avinu – Abraham, our father
Baal Teshuva – a penitent. One who returns to one's roots
Badatz – Rabbinical Court. Superior level of Kashrut blessings
Bagrut – Israeli matriculation exams
Balagan – a real mess!
Bar Mitzva – coming of age ceremony for a boy of thirteen
Baruch Hashem(s) – Blessed be the Lord; *(s)* refers to lots of blessings
Be'ezrat Hashems – Please God; *(s)* means "Please God" many times over
Beit Knesset – synagogue
Bimah – platform, the center stage in a synagogue
Bnei Adam – sons of Adam, humans (i.e. good people)
Bnei Akiva – sons of Akiva; a religious Youth Movement
Bochers – boys
Chagim – religious holydays
Challah – platted bread
Chametz – unleavened bread
Chilonim – secular Jews
Chol – banal
Cholent – a Sabbath stew that keeps warm on a hot plate over Shabbat

Chug – extra curricular activity
Chup – scoop
Chuppa – Jewish marriage ceremony
Chutzpa – the nerve
Daled-amot – refers to the confines of one's home; 4-square meters
David HaMelech – King David
Daven – pray
Din vecheshbon – accountability
Dinim – laws
Doss – a somewhat derogatory term for Haredi people, ridiculing (Yiddish)
Dvar Torah – an explanatory talk on a religious text
Eretz Israel – the land of Israel
Eshet Chayil – woman of worth prayer said by a husband to a wife on Friday night (sometimes spelt Hayil)
Freir – fool
Frum – religious
Gemara – Rabbinical commentary on Mishnah, forming 2nd part of Talmud
Gevalt – beware a Yiddish vernacular for "help"
Gezel Da'at – stealing consciousness
Goyim – gentiles (nations other than the Jewish one)
Habonim – secular Jewish youth group (literal meaning the builders)
Halacha – Jewish law
Halachic – Jewish legal opinion
Hamelech – the king
Hanukka – Feast of Lights
Hardal – acronym for Nationalist Haredi refers to religious Jews who classify themselves somewhere between Modern and Haredi ideology
Hardkoppig – Dogmatic (Afrikaans)
Haredi(m) – ultra religious; (plural)
Haredim le dvar Hashem – mindful to the wish of G-d
Hashem – a term used when referring to G-d. It means: The Name
Hashgacha – supervision; a level of quality control for Kashrut
Hashkaf(ic) – religious perspective

Hassidim – Sect of ultra-religious Jews
Hatikva – hope; the name of the Israeli national athem
Hatzala – a religious emergency response team
Hazar Betshuva – he who became religious
Hiddush – Organization promoting religious freedom and equality
Ikkar and Tefel – principal and secondary
Ima – mother
Ish – man
Ish ha Sade – a man of the field
Ish tam – a simple man of integrity
Jallabiya – long robe/gown worn by traditional Arabs
Kabbalat Shabbat – Prayers that greet the Jewish Sabbath
Kacha Zeh – that's what it is
Kaddish – a prayer recited by the mourner of the deceased
Kaddosh – holy
Kamocha – like yourself
Kashered – made "kosher"; cleaned according to religious custom
Kashrut – the religious rules pertaining to food
Kedoshim – holy
Kedusha – Holiness
Kein anhora – without the evil eye
Kein yirbu – may they multiply
Ki Mitzion Teitsei Torah – For out of Zion comes the Law
Kibitzers – people sitting around and talking
Kibitzing – chatting
Kiddush – benediction over wine
Kippa(ot) – head covering(s)
Kittel – white prayer robe
Klal Israel – the unified body of the nation of Israel
Kneidles – Matza balls
Kohanim – High Priests
Kol Ha'isha – a woman's singing voice
Kol Hakavod – Bravo! Good for you!
Kosher Lemehadrin – super-kosher, kosher over all other certifications
Kosher-lePesach – Kosher for Passover
Krechtzens – complaints

Lag Ba'Omer – a holiday on the 33rd day between Passover and Pentecost
Laila tov – good night
Lechaim – to life. Jewish reverence to life when raising a cup of wine
Le'hefech – on the contrary
Lemehadrin – for the rigorously religious
Leumi(m) – Nationalist; religious with Nationalist sympathies
Leviim – High Priests
Ma(o)shiach – messiah
Machatonistin – In-law
Machmir – a stringent approach to religion
Madrich(im) – counselor(s)
Maidel – a young woman
Makolet – small grocery store
Masechtot – tractates of the Mishna
Mashgiach – person who checks whether food is kosher
Matzot – an unleavened bread Jews eat at Passover
Mea She'arim – One hundred gates; the name of a religious area in Jerusalem
Medaber, Chai, Tzome-ach – akin to the food chain; the human who speaks, the animal, plant life
Menschen – men of integrity
Mephasel – Sculptor
Meshuganas – senseless, crazy behaviors
Mesirat Nefesh – dedication and self-sacrifice
Midda(ot) – virtuous behavior
Mikve – a ritual bathhouse
Minhag – traditions passed down throughout the generations
Minyan – A prayer quorum – a minimum of ten Jewish males over thirteen years old
Mishna – the written version of the Oral Law
Mitzva(ot) – Commandment(s)
Moshe Rabbeinu – Moses our Teacher
Motek – honey; term of endearment
Nefesh – a person; colloqually used as "soul or spirit"

Negiah – touch, usually refers to not having physical contact between the sexes before marriage
Neshama – soul
Neturei Karta – very strict religious sect
Ne'ilah – final prayer of The Day of Atonement, Yom Kippur, literally 'to lock' this comes before neshama
Nidda – untouchable, the time of month a woman menstruates
Noodged – encouraged/whined
Olim – those who ascended to Israel, or moved to live here
Parashat Hashavua – the portion of the week read from the Torah
Parnassa – earning a living
Passuk – Verse
Pesach – Passover
Peulah – Activity
Pirkei Avot – Ethics of the fathers, a manual of behaviors written by the sages
Piyus – reconciliation
Plonta – an impossibly tangled knot
Psak Halacha – religious ruling
Psolet – extraneous
Rabbi Ovadia Yosef (z"l) – Former chief rabbi of Israel's Sephardic Jewish community
Rogelach – sweet pastry
Sabba – grandfather
Sabra – an individual born in Israel also a prickly cactus fruit, rough on the outside and sweet on the inside.
Schach – covering for the Succa
Schita – ritual kosher slaughter
Sefer Shemot – the book of Exodus
Selichot – prayers recited the days before the Jewish New Year. The word refers to entreating G-d to pardon us for our sins
Shaatnez – mixture, the prohibition of using different types of material in the same garment (wool and linen)
Shabbat Shalom – Good Sabbath
Shabbatot – Sabbaths

Shabbos Dvar Torah – a lesson in Torah given during the Sabbath
Shabbos(t) – Sabbath, East European pronunciation of Shabbat this goes before Shabbos Dvar Torah
Shacharit – morning prayers, the first of 3 daily prayers
Shalom – peace, proverbially "hello" or "goodbye"
Shalom Bayit – peaceful home, usually refers to matrimonial harmony
Shavua Tov – have a good week
Sheitel – a wig worn for modesty
Shemot – Exodus
Shfela – lowlands
Shidduch – marriage broker
Shlita – *She yichye le orech yamim tovim ve shlemim* – That he should live long, fulfilled and complete days
Shmatte – a rag
Shmura – ultra-kosher matzot
Shockel – rock back and forth in prayer (Yiddish)
Shomer (shomrei) Shabbat – religiously observant of the Sabbath
Shtupp – stick (Yiddish)
Shuk – market
Shul – synagogue
Siddur – Jewish prayer book
Sikarikim – very strict religious sect
Sinat Chinam – empty, futile animosity
Succa – Tabernacle
Sur Mi'ra Ve'ase Tov – Refrain from evil and do good
Tallis – prayer shawl
Tanach – acronym for Toah, Neviim (the Prophets) and Ktuvim (historical documentation the Hebrew Bible
Tefilat haderech – a prayer recited before embarking on a long journey
Tehillim – psalms
Teshuva – Repentance
Tikkun Olam – repair of what is broken in the world
Toldot Aharon – very strict religious sect
Torah – The Old Testament; The Five Books of Moses
Torah umada – Torah and Science
Treif – not Kosher

Tush – bum
Tzphira – siren
Ve'ahavta Lere'acha Kamocha – love your neighbor as you love yourself
Ve'od eich – and how
Walla – appropriated Israeli slang (from Arabic) which signifies pleasant surprise
Yerida – leaving the Land of Israel to live elsewhere
Yeshiva(ot) – place of religious learning, plural
Yeshiva bochers – (boys) men who attend Yeshivot
Yetzer Hara – the evil inclination
Yid – A Jew
Yiddishkeit – Judaism in Yiddish
Yishuv – settlement
Yom Ha'atzmaut – Independence Day
Yom Kippur – Day of Atonement
Yoshev – polite word for rear end
Zelem Elokim – in the form, in the image of G-d
Zmirot – songs and hymns sang to commemorate love of G-d